International Association for the Integrational Study of Language and Communication

Recent publications (complete list at end)

2022

John Orman. *Indeterminacy and Explanation in Linguistic Inquiry: Contentious Papers 2012 – 2018.*

Adrian Pablé, Cristine Severo, Sinfree Makoni, Peter Jones (orgs.) *Integrationism and Language Ideologies.* (Published in association with Fórum Linguíst!co, Florianópolis, Brasil)

2023

Talbot J. Taylor. *Linguistic Analysis and Normativity. Collected Papers,* vol. 1.

Talbot J. Taylor. *Folk Linguistics, Epistemology, and Language Theories. Collected Papers,* vol. 2.

Talbot J. Taylor. *Children Talking About Talking: The Reflexive Emergence of Language. Collected Papers,* vol. 3.

Talbot J. Taylor. *On the History of Linguistics: Essays of Appreciation and Criticism. Collected Papers,* vol. 4.

Talbot J. Taylor. *Language Origins and Ape Linguistic Research. Collected Papers,* vol. 5.

The International Association for the Integrational Study of Language and Communication

The IAISLC was founded in 1998. It is managed by an international Executive Committee, whose members are:

Adrian Pablé (SUPSI), Secretary
David Bade
Charlotte Conrad (Dubai)
Stephen J. Cowley (University of Southern Denmark)
Daniel R. Davis (University of Michigan)
Dorthe Duncker (University of Copenhagen)
Jesper Hermann (University of Copenhagen)
Christopher Hutton (University of Hong Kong)
Peter Jones (Sheffield Hallam University)
Nigel Love (University of Cape Town)
Sinfree Makoni (Penn State University)
Rukmini Bhaya Nair (Indian Institute of Technology)
Talbot J. Taylor (William & Mary)
Michael Toolan (University of Birmingham)

IAISLC – "In the beginning…" (from left): T.J. Taylor, H. Davis, M. Toolan, R. Harris, N. Love, C. Hutton, D. Davis and G. Wolf

TALBOT J. TAYLOR

FOLK LINGUISTICS, EPISTEMOLOGY, AND LANGUAGE THEORIES

Collected Papers Volume II

Edited by David Bade

www.integrationists.com

International Association for the Integrational Study of
Language and Communication

This collection ©2023

Acknowledgements

"Language constructing language: the implications of reflexivity for linguistic theory". Originally published in *Language Sciences*, vol. 22, no. 4, pps. 483-499, 2000.

"Language in its own image: on epilinguistic and metalinguistic knowledge" Originally published in *Penser l'histoire des savoirs linguistiques*, (S. Archaimbault, ed.), Editions de l'Ecole Nationale Supérieure, 2014.

"Folk-linguistic fictions and the *explananda* of the language sciences". Originally published in *New Ideas in Psychology*, vol. 42, pp. 7-13, 2016.

"Why we need a theory of language" Originally published in *Linguistics and Philosophy: The Controversial Interface* (Harré and Harris, eds.), Oxford: Pergamon, pps.233-48, 1993.

"Folk psychology and the Language Myth". Originally published in *The Language Myth in Western Culture* (R. Harris, ed.) London: Curzon Press, 2002.

"Talking about what happened". Originally published in *Language and History* (N. Love, ed.). London: Routledge. 2006.

"Metalinguistic truisms and the emancipation of the language sciences". Originally published in *Language Sciences*, vol. 61, pp. 104-112, 2017.

Photograph facing the title page: Rita Harris.

Contents

I. Language constructing language: the implications of reflexivity for linguistic theory..................7

II. Language in its own image: on epilinguistic and metalinguistic knowledge..................37

III. Folk-linguistic fictions and the *explananda* of the language sciences..................51

IV. Why we need a theory of language..................77

V. Folk psychology and the Language Myth..................97

VI. Talking about what happened..................121

VII. Metalinguistic truisms and the emancipation of the language sciences..................147

I

Language constructing language: the implications of reflexivity for linguistic theory[1]

Abstract
The reflexive (metalinguistic) properties of language are typically represented as supplemental and inessential. Language, so the story goes, could get along perfectly well without them. The characteristics of language are independent of reflexive discourse — independent of how in metadiscourse we talk about language and its characteristics. This paper challenges this web of received opinion by asking: What might 'first-order' language be like if there were no way to talk, write, or sign about it — that is, if there were no 'second-order' metalanguage? By considering the consequences for writing, translation, pragmatics, semantics, and language acquisition and evolution, the conclusion arrived at is that without 'second-order', reflexive properties, 'first-order' language itself could not exist.

---

[1] This article is a revised version of a paper presented at a monthly meeting of the Chicago Linguistic Society, May 1998. My thanks go to Elaine Jones Francis for the invitation and for her friendship.

What if there were no reflexive language? If no language had any reflexive properties? Or to put it another way: What if we did not have and had never developed any metalinguistic vocabulary or metadiscursive techniques for talking about our language and its everyday uses – the language that is sometimes called, our 'primary' or 'object' language? What would be the consequences?

This paper is intended as a thought-experiment. Its goal is not one of proving any claim or set of claims, nor even of providing an argument. As a thought-experiment, most of the paper consists in posing counterfactual questions and then speculating about possible answers to those questions. Few if any of the answers proposed could be *shown* to be true, or even given any empirical *evidence*. But that is not the point of posing the questions or proposing speculative answers to them. Instead, my aim is to suggest a different way of looking at something that is quite familiar and that we think we already know perfectly well – language. I am fully aware that the picture of language that this method allows me to draw will strike most readers as counter-intuitive, implausible, and perhaps even absurd. Nevertheless, my hope is that the experience of trying to make sense of language in this way can help us break free of the rhetorical compulsion to see our familiar account of the properties of language as *necessary,* as the only account that *could* make sense of all that we 'know' about language. (For a discussion of this rhetorical method and of the motivation for using it, see Taylor, 1992, chap. 1 & 11). If the result is that the proposed shift of aspect in how we see language strikes many readers as disorienting and strange, so much the better.

Another approach would have been to lay out an argument for the importance of reflexive discourse: its importance to the learning of language, to the evolution of language and its everyday uses, to the sociopolitical issues which it raises, and to its description, analysis, and theorization. I have been presenting this argument, bit by bit, point by point, in various papers and books published over the past 20 years (see especially Taylor 1981, 1986, 1990a,b, 1992, 1993, 1997; Shanker and Taylor, 2001). But while my goal here is both more speculative and suggestive, at the same time its focus is much more generalized.

So I begin by asking the reader to imagine the consequences if we users of a language (and in most cases I will be taking English for purposes of illustration) did not have at our disposal any everyday reflexive *vocabulary*, such as the ordinary English words

mean	talk	speak
understand	tell	nonsense
word	promise	agree
say	answer	suggest
refer	describe	reply
true	explain	question
false	ask	request
name	language	justify

How would our experience and use of language be affected if, mysteriously, these words and our capacity to invent them somehow disappeared? I will speculate about some possible consequences below. And yet this thought-experiment should not be limited to imagining a world without metalinguistic vocabulary. For such vocabulary is only the small tip of the reflexive-linguistic iceberg. As with all language, what matters much more than the vocabulary itself, of course, is how we use it. The importance and function of reflexive language will never become clear if we think only in terms of the vocabulary items which are employed in reflexive discourse.

Analogously, we could learn little about the role and influence of ethical discourse in a given society simply by studying the vocabulary used in that discourse – no more than we would learn about the game of soccer if we merely examined the ball, the goal posts, the shoes, and clothes used in the game.

Therefore, to take another step closer to where the real 'action' is in linguistic reflexivity, the reader might reflect on the consequences if there were no metadiscursive *forms of expression* – by which I mean the somewhat routinized phrases for talking about language and our uses of it. The following commonplace expressions are some typical English examples.

"That's what she said."
"Yes, that's right."
"What did he mean by that, anyway?"
"Why did he say that?"
"I'm talking about the one on the left."
"Will you explain that?"
"Sorry, could you say that again?"
"What's that called?"
"Did she understand what you said?"
"Is this what you're referring to?"
"What does comely mean?"
"I'll try to describe it to you."
"That's not true!"
"I don't agree with her."
"What's his name?"
"I insist on doing it this way."
"Please don't lie to me."
"I believe you."
"Promise me you won't go."
"Really?"
"He said he was sorry."
"I'm glad to hear it."

"She ordered me to leave."
"Would you ask him to shut up?"

To take yet one more step closer to the real 'action', we might ask what the consequences would be if we language-users were not just lacking in reflexive vocabulary and forms of expression, but had no metadiscursive means at all for talking reflexively? In other words, if we had no conversational techniques or language games whatsoever for talking about, referring to, commenting on, expressing our disagreement with, criticizing, proposing an interpretation of, questioning, explaining, asking for clarification of, (etc.)... something that we or someone else had said or written or signed? What if we couldn't ask "Who said so?" or "Why do you say that?" or "Don't you agree?" or "How do you know that?"

Another way of raising these general kinds of questions is to ask what the consequences might be if we did not have:

The concept of 'what (someone) said'
The concept of 'what (someone) meant'
The concept of 'what (someone) is/was talking about'
The concept of 'saying (something) again'
The concept of 'understanding (or not-understanding) what (someone) said'
The concept of 'what a particular word/utterance means'
The concept of an utterance 'being true' (or 'being false')
The concept of 'why (someone) says (something)'
The concept of 'explaining (something)'
The concept of 'what (something) is called'
The concept of 'reference'
The concept of 'description'
The concept of 'agreeing'
The concept of a 'name'

The concept of 'lying'
etc., etc.

Many if not all of these concepts would appear to be essential not only to the practical use of language and to making sense of its use by others, but also to the day-to-day management of our cultural lives.

However, before beginning to explore in more detail what might be entailed by the loss of the reflexive remarks by which these concepts are said to be expressed, it is important to note that this topic and these questions are hardly ever raised by theorists of language. The typical assumption appears to be that reflexive discourse is a superficial *supplement* to language itself, one which could be removed without seriously affecting language. A few theorists might concede that this imagined absence of all reflexive forms of language would make a significant difference to particular cultural *uses* of language, all the while insisting that *language itself* does not require reflexive features. In other words, the standard view is that, even if we were bizarrely lacking in all of these metalinguistic words, forms of expression, and language games, we would still have the *concepts* which they express — or at least the concepts which are most crucial to the existence and functioning of language. Naturally, there would be some disagreement about what those crucial concepts are, but it is a good bet that some version of each of the following would be included in most accounts: the concepts of 'meaning', of a 'word', of 'being true', of 'understanding', of 'talking *about*' (or 'referring' to) something, of 'what (something) is called', of 'saying (something) again', and so on. And therefore these language theorists would argue that even if, for instance, we had no such expression as "The word W means X" or no discursive means at all of asking what something means, we could still grasp the relationship/fact expressed by that metalinguistic phrase: that is, we would still have the concept of 'meaning'. After all, these theorists might say, if we did not have the concept of 'meaning', how could we possibly understand that a given word means just what it does: e.g., that *comely* means 'pleasant to look at'? The concept of 'meaning' is too crucial to language, its use, and its understanding—even at the very earliest developmental stages—to depend on its expression in reflexive exchanges.

If pressed to support this assumption, many language theorists will point out that, the world over, infants learn their and other people's names, the meanings of many words, what countless things are called, that some utterances are true and others false, etc., long before they show any mastery of metalinguistic vocabulary. How could children do this unless they had already come to grasp some version of these crucial metalinguistic concepts – unless the linguistic identity of language were somehow already immanent in the phenomena themselves? For instance, John Searle adopts a version of this position in his book *The Construction of Social Reality* (Searle,1995; cf. discussion in Love 1999). Language, he says, is "self-identifying". He argues that institutional facts such as money, property, marriage, etc., require language — indeed "are constituted by" language. However, he claims that language is the exception to this. For, although also institutional, linguistic facts — such as the fact that comely is a word of English or that it means 'pleasant to look at' — do not require language. Language does not require (meta)language in the same way that other institutional facts do. Instead, language is

> precisely designed to be a self-identifying category of institutional facts. The child is brought up in a culture where she learns to treat the sounds that come out of her own and others' mouths as standing for, or meaning something, or representing something. And this is

what I was driving at when I said that language doesn't require language in order to be language because it already is language. (Searle, 1995, p. 73)

A different but related version of what I will call the "Immanency Thesis" is advocated by those linguistic nativists who take metalinguistic concepts such as 'meaning', 'understanding', 'word', etc. to be innate — part of the human genetic endowment (e.g., Pinker, 1994). Thus the generative linguist represents the child as coming into the world equipped with and predisposed to apply such metalinguistic concepts to the vocal and gestural behavior produced around them: e.g., to recognize that the sounds mother produces are 'language' and that they are therefore endowed with 'meaning' and 'structure'.

For language theorists such as Searle and Pinker, who adopt the Immanency Thesis, the mysterious disappearance of reflexive vocabulary and forms of expression would not make much of a difference to the language which the child eventually learns. Linguistic reflexivity — metalanguage and metadiscourse — has, from their point of view, no role in the process of acquisition; nor indeed is it a crucial component of language. Reflexive language is a peripheral, supplementary feature of language, the disappearance of which might affect many of the particular cultural *uses* that we make of language but not *language itself*, the properties of which are self-identifying.

However, it is not my intention here to develop an argument against the Immanency Thesis. Parts of this argument may be found in my publications cited above. Instead, for most of this paper I will put the Immanency Thesis to one side in order to continue with a thought-experiment that does *not* take for granted the self-identifying or innate character of linguistic properties. In support of the thought-experiment performed in this paper, there is the following lesson from history: many forms of scientific pursuit have achieved their greatest advances when their practitioners decided to suspend belief in what had previously been assumed to be the most crucial properties of their object of investigation. In the conclusion, I will briefly return to compare the implications of each version of the Immanency Thesis with those of the claim that the properties of language are reflexively constructed.

Perhaps what first comes to mind as a necessary consequence of a world without linguistic reflexivity is that no language could have a written form. For how could we have the cultural practice of writing if we could not verbally *refer* to a word or utterance, nor make such (e.g., English) reflexive remarks as "You write it like this", or "Write down what she says", or "What does this say (or mean)?", or "Read this"? The existence of any form of writing is fundamentally dependent on the use of reflexive remarks of these general types. The practice of written communication requires that we be able to communicate to each other about meanings, about the written forms themselves, and about the practices of reading and writing. At the same time, the activities involved in *learning* to read and write rely on the use of these and many other reflexive linguistic expressions and techniques. The invention, maintenance, and spread of a writing system in a given community, as well as its day-to-day management as an effective communicational tool, all require the use of reflexive language. (Indeed, as Nigel Love points out to me, without reflexivity, it would be impossible to transfer language from any medium to another: speech to writing, speech to gestural signs, writing to braille, etc. And of course, the same point applies to translating one language into another.) We make writing what it is for 'us' in a given culture — and we keep it that way (or change it) — by talking (and writing) about it in particular ways.

One implication of this point is that because the particular ways that we talk about writing are culturally variable, therefore what writing *is* for the members of one culture should not be assumed to be the same for the members of a different culture. Nor, furthermore, should we assume that there are universal, culture-independent principles of 'what writing is', or culture-independent criteria which determine whether a particular graphic practice is or is not *writing*. (Whether it is what we in Anglophone culture would typically *call* "writing" is another matter.) Because the modern 'linguistic' study of writing is a Western cultural invention, it has been profoundly influenced by the reflexive practices within which alphabetic writing is talked about, maintained, and taught in Western culture. One consequence is that it has often been assumed that every form of writing *must* be conceived by its users as a way of visually representing spoken language and as composed of parts which individually represent particular words or parts of words (see Harris, 1986, 1995). Both of these assumptions are legacies of the lay and pedagogical practices which make writing what it is for those brought up within the Western cultural tradition. However, other cultures talk about and so 'make sense' of writing in other ways (see, for example, Gundaker, 1998; Basso, 1974; Dalby, 1970; Boyarin, 1993). Furthermore, a culture can change its familiar reflexive ways of talking about writing, for instance in response to technological innovations (see Eisenstein, 1983; Olson, 1994; Smalley et al., 1990). Writing requires — is constructed by — reflexive linguistic practices; but this does not mean that all forms of writing are constructed by the familiar reflexive practices on which Western writing depends.

A related consequence to the impossibility of writing without reflexive language is that, without reflexive language, there could not be any standardized languages, such as those commonly recognized today. For while it is debatable whether the process of standardization necessarily requires that the language have a written form (see Joseph, 1987; Milroy and Milroy, 1985; Silverstein, 1996), it certainly does require that the language users be able to talk about, characterize, evaluate, recommend, prescribe, ask questions about, and refer to language. How could there be correct, or incorrect ways of speaking if we had no means of characterizing a form of utterance as 'correct' or 'incorrect'? If we could not say "How is this said?", "What's the right way of saying this?", or "It's *isn't*, not *ain't*"? How could there be the crucial concept of a particular word or phrase being or not being (e.g.) English? (As in "I see what you mean here, but it's just not English!") In other words, the formation and application of evaluative notions, those that are sometimes called matters of "language quality", and of the normative practices that enforce them (Cameron, 1995), clearly depend on the use of reflexive language. Without linguistic reflexivity, there could be no language policies or language planning, no linguistic prescription, no language mavenry, no language politics, and no national ideologies of language (see Schiefflin et al., 1998; Schiffman, 1996; Crowley, 1996).

Now for a different, albeit related question: How far could human language have evolved without the use of reflexive discourse? Could there have evolved a *homo loquens* who was not at the same time a *homo meta-loquens*?

Naturally, this question sounds somewhat paradoxical — as if the suggestion were that early humans could not have developed 'primary' language (language itself) until they had first developed a higher order language, a metalanguage, for talking about primary language. Of course, one might then want to ask: "Well, if that's true, then how could they have developed metalanguage until they had first developed meta-metalanguage for talking about metalanguage?" The absurdity of the regress is obvious.

A first step in reducing the paradoxical appearance of this question is to see how much it depends on what we are willing to call "language". In other words, we could begin by pointing out that humans could never have developed a form of vocal or gestural behavior that would be *recognizable to us as language* if they had not developed the means of making reflexive remarks about that behavior: remarks such as the English "THIS is a hand", "Do you understand?", "What does she *mean*?", "Say that again", "Really?", and "That's what I am talking about". A form of communicational behavior in which it was not possible to say these (or any of the countless other reflexive remarks that the languages of the world make possible) would not seem to us to be the same sort of thing that we today call "language".

Yet this is not because a form of communicational behavior that was similar to modern languages—except that it lacked any reflexive properties—would strike us as so very bizarre. And in any case, this is not the point. Much more important is the possibility that such a form of communicational behavior could not itself possess any of the most salient properties possessed by all those that we call "language". In other words, the only form of communicational behavior that humans could have developed without such reflexive practices not only would not be recognizable to us as language, it also would not have the properties that characterize all known human languages. With any human language, speakers can do all or most of the following sorts of things: refer to objects and events, mean particular things by their words, say what someone else said (or what they themselves said before), perform particular illocutionary acts such as questioning and answering, understand or misunderstand what someone says, agree or disagree with a speaker, truly or falsely describe 'the way things are'. But any form of communication in which reflexive discourse was not possible could not itself possess the crucial properties that make it possible for a language to be a vehicle for such activities.

For example, how could early humans have begun to have gestures or vocalizations that had *particular* meanings before there were any reflexive ways of saying or asking what a given gesture or vocalization meant, of speaking of it as meaning (or indeed, as *not* meaning) such-and-such, etc.? That is, how could such a gesture or vocalization have meant *just THIS* or *just THAT*, in the way that, say, we characterize the English word *cautious* as meaning not 'nervous' or 'frightened', but 'careful to avoid danger'? If there were no reflexive forms of discourse, it is difficult to conceive how any gesture or vocalization could have been endowed with this semantic property. And yet every human language surely has words and utterances which mean *something in particular*, do they not?

At the same time, early humans could not have begun to have gestures or vocalizations that referred to particular objects or events *before* they made use of any reflexive ways of saying or asking what those gestures referred to, or what the speaker was talking about, or whether she was talking about *THIS* or about *THAT* – in the way that in English we say what a word or utterance is *about* or what it refers to. Even more disorienting, it would also seem impossible for hearers to have *understood* anything that speakers said before these communicators possessed the discursive means of constructing the reflexive distinction between understanding and not- (or mis-) understanding. Or to put this counter-intuitive suggestion another way: it is not clear how a hearer's response to something said could have *counted* as a case of understanding or of not-understanding—at least not in the sense that English speakers today speak of understanding and not-understanding—before there were reflexively applicable criteria by which speakers and hearers could determine (explain, and justify) which category a response should count as an instance of. And if there were no possible means of drawing a distinction between *H understanding what S said* and *H not understanding what S said*, then in what sense could that distinction have existed at all? It is surely a form of the ethnocentric fallacy to assume that the reflexive linguistic distinctions which our culture applies in evaluating and characterizing communicational behavior *must* also be applied—and if not explicitly, then implicitly—by the members of every culture. Given this, then in the imagined circumstances of early humans without any reflexive forms of discourse at their disposal, is it not the same fallacy to assume that they must have been applying our reflexive distinctions, albeit only implicitly or unconsciously?

Perhaps we imagine that reflexive distinctions were—or currently are—made which *differ* from those made by English speakers today, yet which had/have a homologous interactional function. However, it would seem that no such reflexive distinction could possibly exist (or have existed) as an interactional or phenomenological reality for a community of speaker-hearers if it were not reflexively constructed and applied in everyday metadiscourse.

Nevertheless, I want to emphasize that this is *not* to say that gestures and vocalizations could not have served various important interactional and communicational functions before there were reflexive means of talking about them as, e.g., "meaning M", "referring to R", "being a repetition of U", or "being true". *Nor* is it to say that such gestures or vocalizations, or their communicational functions, should not be thought of as precursors to the signs and meanings of languages today, or that there must have been some fundamental or unbridgeable evolutionary discontinuity between them and the forms of modern languages. On the contrary, I would argue that such gestures and vocalizations did have important communicational functions and that they were the precursors of the language forms we know today. This is not, however, the position that I have chosen to defend here (although see Taylor 1997, chap. 13). My only goal in this article is to raise the question whether it makes sense to conceive of a gesture or vocalization having a particular property—such as being a word of some particular language and having some particular meaning —before there were the reflexive means to talk about the gesture or vocalization, its meanings, and its uses.

I also want to emphasize that my point is *not* (or not merely) that we late 20th- and early 21st-century humans would expect the legendary 'first inventors of language' to have been able to utter such reflexive remarks and that, if we discovered that they were not able to so, *we* would refuse to apply *our* reflexive term "language" to what they were doing. What I *am* suggesting is that if they were not able to engage in any reflexive linguistic practices, then their communicational behaviour could not have had the semiotic, cognitive, and interactional characteristics that not only characterize all known instances of language but also appear to be essential to the functioning of any form of behavior *as language*. It might therefore be more to the point to say that we modern humans would not recognize such a form of behavior as language *because it would not have been language.*

There is nothing that prevents anyone from using the word *language* for a form of communicational behavior in which reflexive discourse is impossible and which therefore has none of the characteristics that reflexivity makes possible. Nor, as Humpty-Dumpty pointed out in *Through the Looking-Glass*, does anything prevent someone from using the word *glory* to mean 'a nice knock-down argument'. But what is at issue in this thought-experiment is *not* what is or is not *correct usage* for the metalinguistic term *language*, but rather the question of what sense it makes to use that term for a form of behavior which its own users do not speak of—and so, do not conceptualize—as possessing any of the kinds of properties in terms of which all known human languages are characterized.

Take the example of personal names. Every language is said to have personal names (Lehrer, 1994, p. 3374). Yet how could a particular vocalization or gesture have become the *first* name? "When was 'ug' merely a vocalization that typically drew a fellow hominid's attention and when did it become his name?" This comic strip brain-teaser trades on the paradoxical character of trying to imagine how people could have had names before it was possible to ask someone's name ("What's your name?"; "What's he called?"), or say that your name is such-and-such ("Hi, I'm Elaine"), or give a name to a new baby, or speak of such-and-such as someone's name, etc. In other words, imagine that there were *no* such reflexive practices in our culture. It then becomes difficult to conceive how there could still *be* names in our culture. It is no less difficult to make sense of the Immanence theorist's claim that, in spite of this absence of reflexive practices, some of the vocalizations we used in this culture were in fact — appearances aside — *still names*. For how could a given sequence of sounds, such as [əle:n], still be the name of a particular person if we had none of the reflexive practices of naming? For there would not be any way that those sounds could be *treated* as someone's name—that they could function in our interactions *as a name*—if our culture had no such word as *name*, or anything similar, and no reflexive practices in which the word was used. A rose may be a rose by any other name; but a name is not a name unless that's what we say it is. (A similar point is made regarding THE pronunciation of personal names in Wolf et al., 1996.)

This question about names may be extended to other properties which we typically attribute to language. For instance, theorists of language typically ascribe the property of being true (or false) to certain types of utterances. Yet could the utterances of early humans have possessed these properties if they had no means of speaking reflexively? What sense can it make to say that some of early man's utterances must nonetheless have been true and others false, even though the speakers and hearers of those utterances had, according to our thought-experiment, no means of talking about the utterances in such terms? In other words, they could not say things like:

No, that's not true.
Yes, that's right.
That wasn't really what happened.
Let's see if that's correct.
Do you really think so?
I agree.
I don't believe you.
Are you sure?
That's a lie!

An utterance that is true or false is typically characterized as standing in a more general kind of relationship to the world, that relationship which in English we characterize as "standing for" or "representing" or "being about". Without this, it makes little sense for the properties of being true or being false to be attribut-ed to an utterance. Yet, again, how could 'the first inventors of language' have conceived of a representational relationship between what they vocalized and particular states of affairs in the world unless they spoke reflexively of those vocalizations as, for example, we speak in English about our utterances as "meaning", "describing", "being about" (etc.) particular objects, events, or circumstances?

    Instead, our thought-experiment requires us to imagine a world in which none of these reflexive remarks — and so therefore none of the reflexive practices which depend on their use — were available. What could it possibly mean to say that, in spite of this absence, many of the utterances said by early man still were true and many false? How can 'the first inventors of language' have *conceived* of their utterances' truth or falsity, if they had no means of talking about truth and falsity? And if they did not themselves conceive of utterances as being true or being false, what sense can it make to say that, all the same, the utterances nonetheless *were* true and false?

Analogously, speaking from within the reflexively constructed perspective of English, it may seem plausible to us to characterize some of a vervet monkey's alarm calls as "true" and some "false" – depending on whether the predator for whom the alarm is appropriate is or is not approaching. But on the assumption that the vervets themselves have no reflexive practices for talking about an alarm, of characterizing it as true or false (correct, right, wrong, etc.), or of saying what predator it refers to or is about, then we should ask ourselves what sense it makes to assert that the vervets nonetheless conceive of their alarms as referring to particular predators or as being true or false. And we should also ask what sense it might make to say that, even if the vervets themselves do not conceive of their alarms in these terms, all the same, the alarms themselves possess the properties of reference, representation, truth and falsity.

This discussion suggests that the development in human communicational behavior of such paradigmatically 'linguistic' properties as reference, truth, and meaning must in some way have occurred *concurrently* with the development of the metalinguistic tools for and practice of reflexive discourse. Being a vehicle of mutual understanding, meaning, referring, being true; vocalizations and gestures would have come to possess such (or similar) properties at the same time as their speakers and hearers came to characterize them in these kinds of ways. If this picture of the evolution of language can be made sense of, the implications for the study of human evolution, animal communication, cognitive development, and language should be clear. And in this connection it is important to remind ourselves of what Saussure said about the object of linguistic inquiry. "The object is not given in advance of the viewpoint: far from it. Rather, one might say that it is the viewpoint adopted which creates the object" (Saussure, 1916, p. 8). Reflection on the role of reflexive language suggests that the 'viewpoint' that creates the object *language* for us—that determines *what* language is for us, in a given culture—is that which, at least in part, we adopt by speaking of language in certain ways. We fashion the viewpoint from which certain vocalizations become 'names' for us (or 'true', or 'about X', or 'not good English'); and we fashion this viewpoint by means of characterizing those vocalizations as names and by integrating those characterizations and those vocalizations into certain kinds of reflexive practices. We make words have the meanings they do by speaking of them as having those meanings and by embedding them within certain kinds of reflexive practices. Human vocalizations, gestures, and visible marks cannot acquire and so do not have the properties of being names or having meanings "in advance of the viewpoint", as Saussure would say. The viewpoint creates the semiotic object and creates it *as* having particular properties: those that we intuitively 'know' (assume, take, intuit) our vocalizations, gestures, and writing to have. Once we recognize the implications of Saussure's point (and I am not saying that Saussure himself recognized those implications), then at the very least we have to conclude that the evolution of language must have depended just as much on the evolution of *that reflexive 'viewpoint'*—what Wittgenstein (1953) called "grammar"—and of the means of communicating and imposing that 'viewpoint', as it did on the evolution of the properties of the vocalizations, gestures, and marks used and of the properties of the users' neurological structures.

How do children acquire new words? How do they store them? What kinds of information must children represent about each word, so they can identify and understand it when they hear it from someone else, and so they can retrieve and produce it when they speak? (Clark, 1995, p. 393).

The acquisition of vocabulary is the component of the child's development of language which has been most thoroughly studied. From the age of a year or so, children are said to begin to acquire new words, at first fairly slowly but then quite rapidly during a period of acceleration (termed the "vocabulary spurt") which typically begins in the last quarter of their second year (Bloom, 1993). By the age of six, children have been said to possess vocabularies of something like 14,000 words, implying that from the beginning of their vocabulary spurt they had added to their word stock at a rate of as much as ten words a day, a pace which continues into adolescence (Clark, 1995, p. 393).

There are, of course, many different theories which purport to explain how children are so rapidly able to "map meanings onto forms", as the process of lexical acquisition is usually characterized (e.g., Clark, 1995, p. 393). However, some theorists have questioned the methods used in measuring rates of word-learning. Bloom (1973, p. 66) points out that children often forget words that they earlier seemed to have acquired. Others argue that the youngest children typically speak not in true *words* but in "holophrases" (Griffths, 1986, p. 280) or that the criteria for counting a word as learned are sometimes vague (e.g., Nelson, 1973). Yet, one question which is never raised is the role of linguistic reflexivity in what the child learns.

What if a child never acquired the ability to participate in reflexive exchanges about language (metadiscourse)? To continue with one of the examples discussed above, imagine a child who is said to have learned his name. Most parents would say that one of the first words a child learns is his name. Yet one might argue that for a child truly to have learned that, say, *Tommy* is his name, he must be able to do more than look up every time when someone says "Tommy". Many dogs respond in this way, but simply responding appropriately to a given vocal stimulus is hardly sufficient justification for the claim that a dog knows that *Rover* is its name. After all, does a dog know what a name is? If not, how can he know that *Rover* is its name? What if the child regularly responds "Tommy" when he is asked "Now what's your name, little boy?" Few parents—or even sceptical language theorists—would deny that the child should be counted as knowing that *Tommy* is his name. And yet, again, there is more to knowing that *N* is your name than simply being able to produce particular sounds in response to a particular stimulus. For many parrots can do as much. But does such a response, albeit correct, mean that the parrot knows that *Tweetie* is its name? For it may be safely assumed that no parrot has acquired the metalinguistic knowledge of *what a name is*. Yet we should ask ourselves what sense it makes to say that a parrot—or a dog, or a child for that matter—knows that *N* is its name and yet does not know *what a name is*?

    In other words, it would appear that acquiring the knowledge that all language-users eventually acquire—that *N* is your name—is misconceived if it is theorized merely as a matter of coming to recognize an association between a certain set of sounds, e.g., [ta:mi], and you. For what the adult knows in knowing that *N* is his name is much more than this. In knowing that *N* is his name he knows what it is, in his languaculture, for *N* to be his name. That is, he is able to participate in reflexive exchanges about names and he can use, or respond appropriately to, remarks like:

"Hi, I'm Tommy."
"My name is Tommy."
"I'm called Tommy."
"Who are you?" ("Tommy")
"Say your name." ("Tommy")
"Are you Tommy?" ("Yes.")
"Is your name Tommy?" ("Yes.")
"Who is the one called Tommy?" ("It's me.")
"Is there a Tommy here?" ("Yes, me.")
"The boy called Tommy will have to leave now." ("OK.")
"You must be Tommy, right?" ("Right.")

It is clear that no dog or parrot could spontaneously produce or respond competently to such reflexive remarks, but that any experienced speaker of English could do so with ease. At the same time, the infant who turns his head when his name is called will typically take a few months more before he finally develops the abilities to participate competently in all such exchanges. Learning one's name involves learning, as Wittgenstein put it, the "post" which names occupy in our culture's reflexive language games (Wittgenstein, 1953, §257). Truly to learn what his name is a child must also acquire the ability to participate in such reflexive language games.

Another aspect of what children learn is "how to do things with words" (Bruner, 1983). Now, children may produce all sorts of verbal behavior, and will probably be charitably interpreted as performing any number of speech acts, long before they manifest any reflexive linguistic awareness of *what* the speech acts are that they are being taken to perform: in other words, long before they can participate competently in the reflexive practices in which the relevant metapragmatic terms are embedded. This is true whether we're talking about the speech acts of 'apologizing', 'teasing', 'describing', or even 'talking about', 'requesting', and 'answering'. A child may well be saying "Sorry" at more or less appropriate moments although she does not yet manifest any reflexive linguistic awareness that doing so in appropriate circumstances counts as 'apologizing', or what those circumstances are, or to whom one should address one's apology, or what it means to apologize in our culture (its interactional and moral implications). But if so, then what sense does it make to say—when she utters "sorry"—that she is performing the speech act of apology? To become a competent member of our 'languaculture' (Agar, 1994), truly to learn to do the things that *we* do with words, she must do more than develop the ability to act in ways that are superficially indistinguishable from our 'primary' verbal behavior. She must develop a competence in the reflexive languacultural practices which are taken to manifest her awareness of what it is she is doing when she speaks. (This argument is developed further in Shanker and Taylor, 2001.)

These reflections on the reflexive character of language-learning apply not only to personal names and speech act terms, but also to common nouns and other kinds of words; and they suggest problems with the very notion of measuring rates of lexical acquisition. Is the acquisition of a word best conceived as something that happens in a short space of time, so that it makes sense to say that yesterday a child had not yet learned the word X but that now today she has? For example, imagine a child who has started to say the word *shoe* in appropriate circumstances: e.g., when observing her mother putting on her shoe, she says "shoe". (And she does not say "shoe" at inappropriate times.) But what if she could not respond appropriately in situations like the following?

> The child is sitting in a room with various objects in view, including her shoe. She is asked "Can you show me the shoe?", or "Do you know what *shoe* means?", or even "Is THAT (pointing) a shoe?" Or when the child says "shoe",

she is asked "Is this what you said?" by a caretaker holding up a shoe. However, in every case she fails to give an appropriate response and gives no sign that she understands the question.

What sense does it make to say of this child that she knows what *shoe* means? *Some* sense, no doubt. It it not my intention to lay down requirements for using the reflexive expression "has learned X", where X is some feature of language such as the word *shoe*, the speech act of apology, her name, etc. And yet it is clear that it makes little sense to say that the child has become truly competent in some feature of the language she is learning until she is able to do a great deal more. And a significant component of what remains to be learned is reflexive. She still has to acquire the 'viewpoint' from which the linguistic object — e.g., the English word *shoe* — is created.

Imagine the child who never learns to participate in *any* reflexive activities, who never masters any of the terms, expressions, exchanges, or techniques of metadiscourse, who never learns to adopt the reflexive 'viewpoint' from which a language is shaped, fashioned, and made into what we intuitively know it to be. What will language be for her? What will she know about language and its properties and features? What will she be able to do with that knowledge? How will it compare to what a normal human child comes to know about her language? The competence (the knowledge) that a child acquires in learning the words, meanings, speech acts, grammar—indeed any of the 'primary' features —of her language cannot be separated from the web of reflexive linguistic abilities into which that competence is securely woven. "The object is not given in advance of the viewpoint".

Those who undergo thought-experiments must eventually come back to reality. And in this case 'reality' consists of the Immanency Thesis, which is the standard assumption in language theory but which, for the most part of this paper, I have purposefully ignored. But if the counter-intuitive picture that I have drawn is found to be too disorienting, then the reader can always choose to return to the theoretical safety of one or other version of that thesis. For, it has to be admitted, no argument or evidence has been provided here that would *oblige* anyone to accept that language is reflexively constructed, or that early humans could not have had words, or meanings, or reference, or languages without at the same time having had metadiscourse, or that children could not acquire language if they did not also learn how to participate in reflexive linguistic practices. And there are clear, institutionally legitimated alternatives to these bizarre ideas about language constructing language.

One such alternative is simply to assume with Searle that language is self-identifying, that the 'viewpoint' from which its properties take shape is somehow emblazoned on the very face of the linguistic phenomena that early humans first developed and that generations of children so easily acquire. Instances of words, of names, of meanings, of symbols, of reference, of truth, of languages just are recognizable *as such*, whether or not this recognition is ever explicitly articulated or communicated in metadiscourse.

Or, on the other hand, one may opt for the nativist alternative of the Immanency Thesis: Pinker's assumption that the 'viewpoint' from which the properties of language emerge—ontogenetically and phylogenetically—is a matter of human instinct, a legacy of a genetic endowment which is unique to *Homo sapiens*. Thanks to their innate endowment with a language organ, children simply 'see' words, names, meanings, reference, and grammar in the vocal or gestural phenomena with which they are bombarded in their infancy. And 'the first inventors of language' —those who, unlike the previous generation, were the first to be endowed with the language organ—they must have done this as well.

Of course, if it is Searle's version of 'reality' to which we opt to return after this thought-experiment, we will have to concede that there is as yet no way of explaining how early humans could have transformed non-linguistic vocalizations and gestures into the specific features of self-identifying language: that is, into those words, names, nouns, verbs, meanings, questions, sentences, etc., which are said to inhabit every human language. And we will have to admit that it still remains unclear how children so easily learn how to recognize these linguistic properties in the 'blooming, buzzing confusion' that surrounds them in their infant environments. Or, if it is Pinker's version of 'reality' which we opt for, we will still have to acknowledge that there is as yet no plausible account of how a neurological language organ could possibly have evolved by natural selection—by the Darwinian method of slight, adaptive modifications to some preexisting feature. (But no matter, since we can fall back on Chomsky's 'monster-mutation hypothesis': the claim that the language organ must have emerged through some 'catastrophic' event. cf. Chomsky, 1988, 1991; Piatelli-Palmarini, 1989; Taylor, 1997.) And if we opt for Pinker's 'reality', we will have to concede that no language organ has yet been found in the human brain and that no part of the human genetic code has yet been isolated as the source of the child's language innate linguistic knowledge.

Another option, of course, is to choose to keep an open mind about how language became what it is, and how, with each new generation, it again becomes what it is to human cultures. This option would entail refusing to take on faith any claims about evolutionary or ontogenetic miracles. And it would shun any version of linguistic 'reality' whose comfortable familiarity is bought at the price of closing off those avenues of research which seek alternatives to the presupposition of miracles. My hope is that the picture drawn here of the reflexive character of language might offer some speculative suggestions for such research.

References

Agar, M., 1994. *Language Shock: Understanding the Culture of Conversation*. William Morrow, New York.

Basso, K., 1974. "The ethnography of writing." In: Bauman, R., Sherzer, J. (Eds.), *Explorations in the Ethnography of Speaking*. Cambridge University Press, Cambridge, pp. 425-432.

Bloom, L., 1973. *One Word at a Time: the use of single utterance words before syntax*. Mouton, The Hague.

Bloom, L., 1993. *The Transition from Infancy to Language*. Cambridge University Press, New York.

Boyarin, J. (Ed.), 1993. *The Ethnography of Reading*. University of California Press, Berkeley.

Bruner, J., 1983. *Child's Talk: Learning to Use Language*. Oxford University Press, Oxford.

Cameron, D., 1995. *Verbal Hygiene*. Routledge, London.

Chomsky, N., 1988. *Language and Problems of Knowledge: The Managua Lectures*. MIT Press, Cambridge.

Chomsky, N., 1991. "Prospects for the study of language and mind." In: Kasher, A. (Ed.), *The Chomskyan Turn*. Oxford, Blackwell.

Clark, E., 1995. "Later Lexical Development and Word Formation." In: Fletcher, P., MacWhinney, B. (Eds.), *The Handbook of Child Language*. Blackwell, Oxford.

Crowley, T., 1996. *Language in History*. Routledge, London.

Dalby, D., 1970. "The historical problem of the indigenous scripts of West Africa and Surinam." In: *Language and History in Africa*. Africana Press, New York, pp. 109-119.

Eisenstein, E., 1983. *The Printing Revolution in Early Modern Europe*. Cambridge University Press, Cambridge.

Griffths, P., 1986. "Early vocabulary." In: Fletcher, P., Garman, M. (Eds.), *Language Acquisition*. Cambridge University Press, Cambridge.

Gundaker, G., 1998. *Signs of Diaspora, Diaspora of Signs*. Oxford University Press, New York.

Harris, R., 1986. *The Origin of Writing*. Duckworth, London.

Harris, R., 1995. *Signs of Writing*. Routledge, London.

Joseph, J., 1987. *Eloquence and Power: The Rise of Language Standards and Standard Languages*. Blackwell, New York.

Love, N., 1999. "Searle on language." *Language & Communication* 19 (1), 9-26.

Lehrer, A., 1994. "Proper Names: Linguistic Aspects." In: Asher, R. (Ed.), *The Encyclopedia of Language and Linguistics*. Pergamon Press, Oxford.

Milroy, J., Milroy, L., 1985. *Authority in Language*. Routledge, London.

Nelson, K., 1973. "Structure and strategy in learning to talk." *Monographs of the Society for Research in Child Development* 38 (1-2, Serial No 149).

Olson, D., 1994. *The World on Paper*. Cambridge University Press, Cambridge.

Piattelli-Palmarini, M., 1989. "Evolution, selection and cognition: from "learning" to parameter setting in biology and in the study of language." *Cognition* 31, 1-44.

Pinker, S., 1994. *The Language Instinct*. Morrow, New York.

Saussure, F., 1916. *Cours de linguistique générale*. Payot, Lausanne and Paris. (Page reference to 2nd ed., 1922). English translation by R. Harris. Duckworth, London, 1983.

Schiefflin, B., Woolard, K., Kroskrity, P.V., 1998. *Language

Ideologies: Practice and Theory. Oxford University Press, Oxford.

Schiffman, H., 1996. *Linguistic Culture and Language Policy*. Routledge, London.

Searle, J., 1995. *The Construction of Social Reality*. Penguin, London.

Shanker, S.G., Taylor, T.J., 2001. "The House that Bruner Built." In: Bakhurst, D., Shanker, S.G. (Eds.), *Language, Culture, Self: The Philosophical Psychology of Jerome Bruner*. Sage, London.

Silverstein, M., 1996. Monoglot "Standard" in America. In: Brenneis, D., Macaulay, R. (Eds.), *The Matrix of Language*. Westview Press, Boulder, CO, USA.

Smalley, W.A., Vang, C.K., Yang, G.Y., 1990. *Mother of Writing: The Origin and Development of a Hmong Messianic Script*. University of Chicago Press, Chicago.

Taylor, T.J., 1981. *Linguistic Theory and Structural Stylistics*. Pergamon Press, Oxford.

Taylor, T.J., 1986. "Do you understand? Criteria of understanding in verbal interaction." *Language & Communication* 6 (3), 171-180 (reprinted in Taylor, 1997).

Taylor, T.J., 1990a. "Which is to be Master? The Institutionalization of Authority in the Science of Language." In: Joseph, Taylor (Eds.), *Ideologies of Language*. Routledge, London (reprinted in Taylor, 1997).

Taylor, T.J., 1990b. "Normativity and Linguistic Form." In: Davis, H. and Taylor, T.J. (Eds.), *Redefining Linguistics*. Routledge, London (Reprinted in Taylor, 1997).

Taylor, T.J., 1992. *Mutual Misunderstanding: Scepticism and the Theorizing of Language and Interpretation*. Durham, NC. Routledge, London.

Taylor, T.J., 1993. "Why we need a theory of language. In: Harré, R., Harris, R. (Eds.), *Linguistics and Philos-*

ophy: the Controversial Interface. Pergamon Press, Oxford, pp. 233-247 (Reprinted in Taylor, 1997).

Taylor, T.J., 1997. *Theorizing Language: analysis, normativity, rhetoric, history*. Pergamon Press, Oxford.

Wittgenstein, L., 1953. *Philosophical Investigations.* Blackwell, Oxford.

Wolf, G., Bocquillon, M., de la Houssaye, D., Krzyzek, P., Meynard, C., Philip, L., 1996. "Pronouncing French Names in New Orleans." *Language in Society*, vol. 25, 3.

II

Language in its own image: on epilinguistic and metalinguistic knowledge

In the introduction to his magisterial 2-volume *Histoire des idées linguistiques*, Sylvain Auroux raises an issue of prime importance to the history of linguistic thought: the relationship between epilinguistic and metalinguistic knowledge (see also Culioli 1968, Gombert 1992).

> Le savoir linguistique est multiple et il débute naturellement dans la conscience de l'homme parlant. Il est épilinguistique, non posé pour soi dans la représentation, avant d'être métalinquistique, c'est-à-dire représenté, construit et manipulé en tant que tel à l'aide d'un métalangage (éléments autonymes et noms pour les signes). La continuité entre l'épilinguistique et le métalinquistique peut être comparée avec la continuité

entre la perception et la représentation physique dans les sciences de la nature. (Auroux 1989, p.18)

The relationship between the epilinguistic and the metalinguistic raises a central issue in our understanding of the nature of linguistic knowledge or competence. Indeed, the importance of this issue is suggested by Auroux only a few lines below the passage quoted above: « Dans le domaine proprement grammatical, encore aujourd'hui, il n'y a pas toujours véritable solution de continuité, peut-être parce que *le langage est un système régulé par sa propre image.* » (p.18 – emphasis added).

Reflection on the implications of this suggestion—that language is constructed and regulated by its own reflexive image—must, I believe, lead us to conclude that the relationship between epilinguistic and metalinguistic knowledge is more complicated than might at first be imagined. To see why this is so, I propose to work through a thought experiment. As a simple, surveyable template for this thought experiment, I will use the builder's language game described in §2 of Wittgenstein's *Philosophical Investigations* (Wittgenstein 1953). In this language game the builder's assistant, B, brings one of four different types of building material to the builder, A, whenever A utters one of the four signs *beam, slab, block*, or *pillar*. Wittgenstein says that this language game should be thought of "as a complete primitive language" (§2). Note, in particular, that no metalinguistic—or, more generally, reflexive—utterances are possible, for the only signs in this language are *beam, slab, block*, and *pillar*. We will not inquire into how this language game came into being, but simply take it for granted, just as Wittgenstein describes it. Each of A's possible utterances is apparently a straightforward sign for the building material in question: that is, the sign *slab* means a slab; the sign *block* means a block; and so on. Alternatively, one might take the sign to mean the idea of the building item in question, or possibly even B's response of bringing the item to A. However, in the context of the present discussion, it is irrelevant which of these albeit very different 'meanings' the builder's signs are taken to have.

Now, in Wittgenstein's description, the practice works well. But what happens if on one occasion, when the builder A produces an utterance, B, the assistant, does not know whether she said "block" or "beam"? What can B do? There are no metalinguistic signs in the language game with which B might initiate a repair, asking A to repeat what she said, or asking whether she said "block" or "beam", or even just saying that he did not understand what she said. Nor can he simply say "You said, 'block', didn't you?" For, *ex hypothesi*, the only utterances possible in Wittgenstein's language game are "block", "slab", "beam", and "pillar". Or consider another possibility: What happens if, although he heard A's utterance clearly, B is still uncertain whether A is asking for a particular beam—just THIS → beam here on the left—or whether she is asking for any old beam? There are no signs in Wittgenstein's language game by which the speaker might be requested to specify her referent. That is, despite his uncertainty, B cannot ask something like "Which beam do you *mean*?" or "Do you *mean* this beam here or just any one?"

In considering these communicational dilemmas, we need to keep in mind that this thought experiment assumes that there are no alternative means by which B or A can express such metalinguistic utterances – by hand gestures, by specific prosodic forms, by facial expressions, by nonverbal grunts, and the like. For if such non- or para-linguistic signs were available to them, that would in effect be to expand the language game beyond Wittgenstein's description of it as "complete". Again, our thought experiment involves a language game in which no metalinguistic remarks are possible; in which case it is no good sneaking them in the back door by allowing their expression to be nonverbal.

Now, suppose that, on one occasion, B notices that A's pronunciation of "beam" holds the vowel for longer than he had been used to hearing, and this leads him to wonder if she means something different by pronunciation? That is, A says [bi::m], instead of the more familiar [bim]. The assistant cannot ask "Does [bi::m] mean something different from [bim]?" or "Is a [bi::m] the same as a [bim]?" Or what if B does not know if A is talking to him or to another worker standing nearby? What can B do? Since the language game has no metalinguistic capacity, he cannot say what one would ordinarily say in such circumstances: that is, ask a question like "Are you talking to me or him?" or "Is it me you are asking?" Or what if, for whatever reason, B is not sure if A is serious or sincere? Perhaps B suspects that A is only pretending to ask for a beam? Still, there is no way to express this uncertainty in the language game and no way to ask A to clarify. Whereas in ordinary circumstances one might say "You're just joking, right?" or "You don't really mean that, do you?" or "Is it true that you want the beam?", this metalinguistic move is not available in Wittgenstein's language game. In sum, it would seem that no explicit means are available to B by which he can clear up these types of communicational confusion. All he can do, in such circumstances of uncertain knowledge, is to stand unresponsively or make an arbitrary choice of one of the possibilities that occur to him.

So far we have only been considering how the lack of a metalinguistic capacity limits the communicational flexibility of B, the hearer. But what about A, the speaker? What, for instance, can A do if she utters "block" but B brings her a slab? In the same situation, one might say "No, I said 'block', not 'slab'" or "You misunderstand. THIS → is what a 'block' is". But these metalinguistic remarks are not possible in

Wittgenstein's language game. Similarly, what if A does not know whether B understood her utterance? She cannot say "I'll say that again" or even simply "Do you understand?", as we might say in the same situation. She can repeat herself, of course, but what she cannot do is to verbally identify what she is doing as "repeating" herself or as "saying it again" and thereby distinguish this repetition of her first command from the issuing of a second command. In other words, like B, A's hands are tied. There is nothing A can do if she is unhappy with B's response to her utterance or if she is not certain whether B understood what she said, whether B was listening, whether B knows which beam she is referring to, whether B knows that [bim] and [b::im] mean the same thing, whether B realizes that she was only joking, and so on. The lack of metalinguistic tools in the language game drastically limits the speaker's possibilities no less than it does the hearer's, even for the extremely limited interactional goals which Wittgenstein's language game is intended to serve.

Another equally important consequence of this lack of metalinguistic possibilities is that the normative or conventional character of the language game would be limited: limited, that is, to the point of disappearance. Because A cannot speak reflexively, she cannot say things like "No, THIS→ is what a beam is" or "When I say 'slab', you should bring me one of these" or even "No, that's wrong" or "Yes, that's right". In other words, without metalinguistic expressions if B makes a mistake, A has no way of correcting him or pointing out what he *ought to* have done or reminding him of what he *should* know about the word. She cannot even identify his mistake as a *mistake*.

Consequently, there is no way for A to hold B explicitly responsible for how he responds to her utterances, for there are no metalinguistic means for expressing this responsibility. At the same time, neither can B hold A responsible for what she said. Suppose that A says "beam", which B promptly brings to her, but A looks unhappy. B cannot respond to the effect "But you told me to bring a beam and this *is* a beam!" In other words, even though Wittgenstein refers to the builders' activity as a language *game*, still, without the possibility of metalinguistic discourse, it cannot *be* anything like what we call a "game" – because it cannot be normative.

Thus far, I have been considering how discourse in Wittgenstein's builder's language is affected by its lack of a metalinguistic capacity – how the practices of playing this language game are affected. But what about the individual signs themselves? On first glance the fact that metalinguistic discourse is not possible in the builder's language does not seem to have any impact on the properties of the signs themselves. After all, there are still four distinct signs: *beam, slab, block*, and *pillar*. The sign *slab* still means a slab; the sign *beam* means a beam, and so on. The absence of a metalinguistic capacity appears only to impact discourse with the signs, but not the very signs themselves. This also seems to be the case if we consider the signs from an epistemic perspective, as suggested by the distinction between epilinguistic and metalinguistic knowledge. Do the builder and his assistant know what the signs mean? Do they have epilinguistic knowledge of the signs' meanings, even though they lack the metalinguistic tools for engaging in discourse about those signs and their meanings? Again, our first inclination is probably to respond that, yes, they do: for instance, they know that the sign *beam* means that thing over there. *Prima facie*, it does not seem relevant to the question *whether they know its meaning* that the content of that knowledge cannot be made explicit in metalinguistic discourse; that is, that there is no way of saying "*Beam* means that" or anything like it.

In what follows, I will present two different objects of comparison whose differing analogical relationships to the builder's language should motivate doubts about the foundational distinction between epilinguistic and metalinguistic knowledge. As the first such object of comparison, imagine the following game. A child is brought up in a non-English-speaking community in which there are no commercial or monetary practices. He undergoes behavioral training in a form of exchange involving candied sweets and four kinds of paper notes: a $1 bill, a $5 bill, a $10 bill, and a $20 bill. We will imagine that the notes have been accidentally dropped from the sky by a passing jetliner. As a result of his training, when the child is handed a $1 note, he passes back a chocolate mint; if he is handed a $5 note (or five $1 notes), he passes back a lemon drop, and so on. But that is all. There is no discourse about the notes, the objects, the practice of buying, or matters of value, being worth, cost, and so on. The game is complete just as I have described it.

In this exchange game, does a chocolate mint *cost* $1? Is *the value* of a lemon drop $5? Is a $5 note *worth* five times more than a $1 note? What sense would it make for us to characterize in this way the items and the relationships-between-the-items in the exchange game? It seems to make some sense, I admit. But my question is not really about the linguistic propriety of using these English commercial terms in this way. On the contrary, the question is whether the notes and sweets do in fact *have* the properties attributed to them: that is, the properties of value, of costing such and such, of being money, of comparative worth, and so on. Are these properties somehow *immanent* in the objects themselves, that is, in the notes and the sweets themselves? Or are they immanent in the actual behaviors produced by the children? Is this the case even though it is impossible in this game ever to talk about value, being worth, costing, money, and so on? Of course, if we decide that it is *not* the case that a $5 note used in this game has a value, or that a $5 note is not worth more than a $1 note, then we have to accept that such a $5 note is not the same kind of semiotic object as the five-dollar bill in my pocket. For the one in my pocket *does* have a value, *is* worth more than a $1 bill, and so on.

Let's examine this example within the epistemic frame. Do the children playing this exchange game *know* that a chocolate mint costs $1? Or that $5 will buy you a lemon drop? Or that a lemon drop is worth more than a chocolate mint? We may, again, have an inclination to say "Yes, they do". For affirming that they know these things helps *us* make sense of the children's actions in the game. But this is a projection from our own reflexive perspective, is it not? For how could the children themselves be aware of these properties of the culturally-dependent practices of commercial exchange, while never having heard any talk of such practices and their component properties? Would it not be absurd to say that the children somehow automatically, "epi-commercially" know these things about the notes and objects in their game? If so, then we have to acknowledge that what *they know* about a $5 note is very different indeed from what *I know* about the one in my pocket.

There are a few points that this constructed analogy to the builder's language should bring into the foreground. For, at first glance, it seems to make sense to say that the signs used by the builder and her mate have meanings, refer to particular objects, are semiotically distinct from one another, can be repeated, and so on. But comparison with the children's exchange game may lead us to doubt whether the signs really do have those properties. No doubt, when the builder says "Block", the assistant fetches a block and brings it to her. But does this fact necessarily entail that the sign has a meaning or reference or that it is the same sign she uttered a moment ago? Other explanations are possible for the participants' actions and responses. We could imagine a dog being conditioned to respond as the assistant does and yet not feel that these responses justify saying of the dog that he understands "the signs' meanings". The sign's possession of those properties is not necessary for the language game to proceed just as Wittgenstein describes it. As regards our initial feeling that the builder's signs have meanings, refer to things, can be repeated, understood, and so on: at the very least, this commonsense response stands in need of justification.

Or, to put this puzzle in an epistemic frame: Do the builder and his mate *know* that the sign *beam* means a particular type of building material? Do they know that the builder's utterance of this sign refers to that object over there? Again, our first response may well be to answer "yes" to these questions, for that response helps *us* to make sense of what happens in the language game. But we have to ask ourselves how the builder or her mate could know these things in the absence of a capacity for metalinguistic discourse: i.e., what knowing these things epilinguistically could possibly consist in? Is it not equally questionable to assume that they automatically and implicitly attribute these semiotic properties to the vocalizations as it is to assume that the children attribute the properties of value, price, being worth, and so on to the notes and objects in the exchange game? From the perspective afforded by this comparison, then, we can see how different the signs in the builder's language are from the signs exemplified by the words familiar to English speakers: *block, beam, slab*, and *pillar*.

Let us now turn to a second object of comparison—one that may help us see the builder's signs in yet another light. As an infant learns about a particular perceptual object, she learns what in the ecological psychology initiated by James Gibson is called the object's "affordances" (1979). Gibson applies the concept of affordances to many kinds of phenomena in the child's developmental environment. For our purposes, hand tools will serve to illustrate the concept. A child's learning about a particular tool is seen as inseparable from learning what the tool is 'good for', what can be done with it: that is, what it affords for action. Learning what a saw is involves learning that it is good for sawing. Similarly, you do not yet know what a drill is unless you know that it is good for making cylindrical holes in objects. As the ecological psychologist Ed Reed puts it: "When one learns about the affordances of things one is learning about properties of objects, events, and places with respect to one's own actions." (Reed 1993, p. 52). Moreover, Gibson argued that cognitive development crucially involves the child's coming to grasp what things afford for others as well as for herself. Thus, ecological psychologists also apply the concept of affordances to sociocultural objects. Reed explains: "a bat affords hitting a ball by seeing it as a component of a complex [cultural] event in which balls are thrown and swung at" (Reed 1993, p. 53).

A verbal sign can also be conceptualized in terms of its affordances. Knowing what *block* means in the builder's language is a matter of knowing what it is 'good for' in that practice. So, the builder knows that *block* is the word to utter in order to have a block brought to her; that this is what this word affords in the language game. And the assistant knows that *block* has this affordance for her. Consider the affordances of a sign used in a verbal practice which—unlike the builder's language—possesses a metalinguistic capacity. Such a sign can be explained; its identity and its meaning can both be queried; its reference can be made more specific ("I mean that block"), as can its addressee ("It's you I am talking to"); it can be characterized as a repetition or a correction of an earlier sign; its production can be characterized as a particular kind of speech act ("I'm asking you, not ordering you"); the speaker's purpose in using it can be characterized as of a particular cultural type ("I'm only teasing".); the hearer's response to it can be characterized as correct or incorrect, a mishearing, a misunderstanding, and so on. These, we might say, are some of the signs' *reflexive affordances* (Taylor 2010). A sign used in a practice without metalinguistic capacities, such as the signs in Wittgenstein's builder's language, does not have reflexive affordances.

Furthermore, because the builder's language lacks the capacity for metalinguistic discourse, its signs cannot have normative properties. There is no way to say things like "That's wrong" or "This is what you should say", or "When X occurs, then you ought to do Y". Metalinguistic remarks of this normative kind are not among a sign's affordances in the builder's language. The result is that the signs in this language game are what we might call "frictionless", a metaphor by which I mean that the properties of a given sign can slide this way or that—freely—with nothing to hold it in place. A may use it or B respond to it arbitrarily, there being no means of applying or manifesting any normative expectations or consequences. In such a language, if Humpty Dumpty decides to use the word *glory* to mean 'a nice knock-down argument', then there simply is nothing Alice can say in reply, and her objection about whether "one *can* make words mean whatever one wants" cannot even be expressed. In other words, in ecological psychology's sense of knowing what an object is 'good for', because the use of a sign in the builder's language cannot be normatively regulated, *it is good for anything whatsoever* – which is to say, for nothing at all.

English, like every other human language, is a verbal practice whose signs do offer all of these reflexive affordances and many, many more. Therefore if, in keeping with this analogy, we picture knowing a sign as involving grasping its reflexive affordances, then what the builder and her assistant know about the sign *block* has to be seen as very different from what English speakers know about the word *block* – or, indeed, from what the speakers of any language know about its words, regardless of their training in literacy or schooling of any kind. To be sure, there is a superficial identity between *block* in English and *block* in the builder's language game—they both sound the same and there is some association with a kind of building material—but because their reflexive affordances are so different, knowing the English word *block* is a wholly different matter from what the builder and her assistant know.

This cursory review of two objects of comparison to Wittgenstein's builders' language may help us to make sense of the following claim regarding the relationship between metalinguistic discourse and linguistic knowledge. It is only because the signs of human language have reflexive affordances that they are as polished, articulated, useful, and precise as we *know* them to be: knowledge which we *count* on in our everyday verbal activities. Signs like those in the builders' language—signs which, because of the absence of a metalinguistic capacity in the language game, have no reflexive affordances—stand proportionately to the signs of human languages as a sharp stick stands to a laser drill. Language is constructed and regulated by its own reflexive image (Taylor 2003). And yet, if we accept that the identity of a human sign stands in an internal relation to its reflexive affordances and that metalinguistic discourse has an essential and ineliminable role in fashioning the parts, powers, and uses that we know human language to have, then we must at the same time acknowledge that different cultures do not all talk the same way as we do about their verbal acts and the linguistic tools with which they perform them. As the attention given by linguistic anthropologists to this topic has shown, the items used in metalinguistic discourse—as well as the relationships between those items—are not structurally isomorphic from language to language, even though the powerful influence of the West's historically institutionalized forms of metalinguistic discourse might incline us to think that they are. And we must go further: for we must also acknowledge that even fellow members of the *soi-disant* "same" culture do not all share equal access or identical positionings relative to their own culture's patterns of metalinguistic discourse (Agha 2007). Nor can we blithely assume that those patterns are matters of implicit consensus and homogeneity. On the contrary, as sociolinguists and historians of linguistic inquiry have been showing us for decades—with Sylvain Auroux very much at the forefront of this effort—these are matters of social differentiation, contestation, mystification, and power.

References

Agha Asif, 2007, *Language and Social Relations*, Cambridge U.K., Cambridge University Press.

Auroux Sylvain, 1989. *Histoire des idées linguistique, tome 1, La naissance des métalangages*. Liège, Pierre Mardaga, p. 13-37.

Culioli Antoine, 1968. « La formalisation en linguistique » *Cahiers pour l'analyse*, n° 9/7.

Gibson James, 1979. *The Ecological Approach to Visual Perception*, Boston, Houghton Mifflin.

Gombert Jean-Emile, 1992. *Metalinguistic Development*, Chicago, University of Chicago Press.

Reed Edward, 1993. "The intention to use a specific affordance: A conceptual framework for psychology", *Development in Context: Activity and Thinking in Specific Environments*, R. Wozniak, K. Fischer eds., Hillsdale, NJ: LEA

Taylor Talbot, 2003. "Language Constructing Language: the implications of reflexivity for linguistic theory", *Rethinking Linguistics*, H. Davis, T.J. Taylor eds., London, Routledge.

Taylor Talbot, 2010. "Where does language come from? The role of reflexive enculturation in language development", *Language Sciences*, n° 32/1, p. 14-27.
Wittgenstein Ludwig, 1953. *Philosophical Investigations*, Oxford, Basil Blackwell.

III

Folk-linguistic fictions and the *explananda* of the language sciences

Abstract
For the past two millennia, the explananda of language theory have been inherited from the Western linguistic tradition. The legacy is what might be called "the Western linguistic imaginary": an indeterminate but deeply mesmerizing inventory of entities, properties, and powers of language commonly attributed to language and language-users and which therefore seem to stand in need of explanation. In recent years, naturalistic research programs in the cognitive sciences have provided illuminating explanations of basic ("lower-order") cognitive phenomena. The challenge today for the science of language is whether, in transforming itself along the lines of epistemological naturalism, it can provide similarly illuminating explanations of any of its traditional explananda. In addressing this challenge, greater attention needs to be given to the source of such explananda in the everyday, culturally-diverse practices of folk metalinguistics.

Some naturalists take a special interest in our everyday or folk commitments. For them, the interesting philosophical project is to determine how much, if any, of what we ordinarily think about various subject matters (e.g. the mental, the moral, the aesthetic) is compatible with our best scientific understanding of what there is. To decide this, special methods have been created for (1) perspicuously representing our folk commitments and (2) examining if these outstrip, or go beyond, the commitments of a certain scientific understanding of what there is in nature. By these lights the philosophical task of the naturalist is to determine if the folk are committed to something over and above what is posited by a certain scientific world view. (Hutto, 2011 'Presumptuous Naturalism', p. 2)

1. Naturalistic language science and the Western linguistic imaginary

The tide is changing in the language sciences. For the past two millennia, the *explananda* of the language sciences have been inherited from the Western linguistic tradition and its many subsidiary practices. This tradition—now massively institutionalized and authoritative—is conventionally traced back to ancient Greece and Rome, although it is important to recognize the continuously regenerative support that the tradition has received and continues to receive from cultural forms of metalinguistic discourse, including the institutionalized and normative practices of teaching language, translating it, writing it, reading it, editing it, 'correcting' and 'improving' it, and so on. This history—and its consequences for the language sciences—have been illuminatingly analyzed and meticulously described in the works of the late Roy Harris, as well as in the writings of many other scholars (Auroux, 1989; Baumann &

Briggs, 2003; Harris, 1980, 1981, 1987; Harris & Taylor, 1997; Linell, 2005; Love, 2004; Reddy, 1979; Taylor, 1992).

An important legacy of this history has been what we might call "the Western linguistic imaginary": an indeterminate but deeply mesmerizing inventory of entities, properties, and powers commonly attributed to language and language-users and which therefore seem, to theorists of language, to stand in need of explanation. It is this cultural legacy of *explananda* that I am calling "folk-linguistic fictions". Under the spell cast by this imaginary, language theorists from Plato to the present day have taken it to fall within their remit to provide explanations of such things as

— what meanings are
— what it is for an expression to refer to something
— what a word is
— what a sentence is
— what a language is
— what a dialect of a language is
— what it is to mean such-and-such by what you say
— what it is to understand what someone has said or written
— what it is to say something about a situation or event
— what it is for two instances of language to be the same word (or same sentence) or to have the same meaning
— what it is for an instance of language to be true
— what it is for an expression to be correctly formed
— what it is for two (or two million) people to be speakers of (to know) the same language
— what it is for two communicational agents—in real time and concrete contexts, individually and in

dialogic groups and time scales—to 'make use' of these entities, properties, and powers.
Etc.

In addition, language theorists have also felt the need to explain how children so rapidly, and apparently without explicit instruction, gain command of these linguistic entities, properties, and powers.

However, in recent years, epistemological developments in the philosophy of mind and the cognitive sciences have put the inherited assumptions about the *explananda* of the language sciences in a new light. Kitchener characterizes the naturalistic epistemology spreading through the cognitive sciences as follows:

> If epistemology is to become thoroughly naturalistic and to employ the scientific method, then it would seem that all epistemological analyses must (in some sense) be *empirical* in nature, countenancing no non-naturalistic entities, no non-naturalistic cognitive faculties, and no non-naturalistic methods. (Kitchener, 2006, p. 79)

Within the cognitive sciences, naturalistic (or "naturalized") research programs have succeeded in providing illuminating explanations of basic ("lower-order") cognitive phenomena. (For an enlightening discussion see Hutto and Myin's *Radicalizing Enactivism: Basic Minds without Content*, 2013) The challenge today for the science of language is whether, in transforming itself along the lines demanded by epistemological naturalism, it can provide similarly illuminating explanations of any of its traditional *explananda*: that is, paraphrasing Kitchener, whether it can do so without countenancing any non-naturalistic entities or properties, without attributing any non-naturalistic powers to acts of language or to language-users, and without employing any non-naturalistic methods.

2. The hard problem of folk linguistic fictions

What, then, are naturalistically-inclined language scientists to do with the fictions that are the legacy of Western culture's linguistic tradition? At least two alternatives present themselves.

One approach is to borrow the eliminativist strategy advocated by some cognitive scientists with regard to the analogous fictions of the folk psychology imaginary, such as the notions of 'belief', 'idea', 'reason', 'wish', 'mental images', and so on (cf. Braddon-Mitchell and Nola, 2009; Churchland, 2007; Greenwood, 1991; Stitch, 1996, Wheeler, 2005). Cognitive eliminativists claim that these notions are "the heritages of a timid savage past", handed down, generation after generation, at mother's knee (Watson, 1924, p. 3) and that they now should be assigned the same fate as was meted out, following the birth of modern chemistry, to alchemical notions such as 'phlogiston', 'caloric', and 'essences'. For instance, the cognitive eliminativists Paul and Patricia Churchland argue that it is physical properties and processes in the brain which should be the ultimate *explananda* for scientific psychology and that folk psychological notions should be eliminated from scientific discourse. "[F]olk psychology is false, and its ontology is chimerical" (Churchland, 1991, p. 65). Another who argues against the reliance on folk psychology in cognitive research is the philosopher Dan Dennett. He illustrates his argument with this colorful thought experiment:

> Suppose we find a society that lacks our knowledge of human physiology, and that speaks a language just like English except for one curious family of idioms. When they are tired, they talk of being beset by fatigues, of

having mental fatigues, muscular fatigues, fatigues in the eyes and fatigues of the spirit. Their sports lore contains such maxims as "too many fatigues spoils your aim" and "five fatigues in the legs are worth ten in the arms". When we encounter them and tell them of our science, they want to know what fatigues are. They have been puzzling over such questions as whether numerically the same fatigue can come and go and return, whether fatigues have a definite location in matter and space and time, whether fatigues are identical with some particular physical states or processes or events in their bodies, or are made of some sort of stuff. We can see that they are off to a bad start with these questions, but what should we tell them? One thing we might tell them is *that there simply are no such things as fatigues* — they have a confused ontology. We can expect some of them to retort: "You don't think there are fatigues? Run around the block a few times and you'll know better! There are many things your science might teach us, but the non-existence of fatigues isn't one of them!" We ought to be unmoved by this retort. (…) Fatigues are not good theoretical entities, however well entrenched the term "fatigues" is in the habits of thought of the imagined society. The same is true, I hold, of beliefs, desires, pains, mental images, experiences—as all these are *ordinarily* understood. Not only are beliefs and pains not good theoretical things (like electrons or neurons), but the *state-of-believing-that-p* is not a well-defined or definable theoretical state. (Dennett, 1981, p. xix-xx)

Now, from the perspective of a naturalistically-inclined language scientist, it is easy to see that, to the Churchlands' and Dennett's list of "bad theoretical entities", one could add those *explananda* of the language sciences that are the legacy of the Western linguistic tradition: e.g., meanings, words, languages, reference, truth, names, understanding, and so on. Of course, to paraphrase Dennett, it is true that the "natives" who populate the linguistic community expect the language sciences to tell them "what these things are": that is, these "things" which are regularly mentioned in everyday metalinguistic discourse about language in their community (e.g., in the Anglophone linguistic community). However, in keeping with Dennett's recommendation for commonsense psychological "things", the naturalist language scientist should not be dissuaded from his eliminativist intentions. For, to put it in Dennett's terms, the natives in the Anglophone linguistic community have a confused ontology. (The same verdict would of course also apply to the natives of the thousands of other linguistic communities worldwide.) Meanings, words, languages, names, acts of reference, and so on are not "good theoretical things (like electrons or neurons)". They are not admissible, as Hutto puts it in the quote at the head of the paper, within "our best scientific understanding of what there is". Such a linguistic ontology is at best a comfortable cultural fiction, but a fiction nonetheless. And a naturalized linguistic science should not be the study of fictions, no matter how entrenched those fictions are in the habits of discourse among the ordinary members of the society. In addition, naturalist language scientists should refrain from characterizing their explanatory objects with folk metalinguistic expressions like "the English language", "meaning", "word", "true", "is about", "name", "implies", "understands", or any of the innumerable cultural variants that may be found in folk metalinguistic practices around the world.

Not surprisingly, many of the theorists who are pioneering the naturalistic turn in the language sciences today draw back from adopting such an eliminativist strategy, at least when taken to such scorched-earth extremes. After all, does it not seem reasonable to expect that a scientific explanation of language should explain what it is to mean something when we speak and what it is for part of what we say—a word—to mean? Or to insist that language science must explain what a word is or what it is for two parts of an utterance (or of different utterances) to be instances of the same word – or to have the same meaning? And does it not seem equally reasonable to demand of language science that it explain what it is for an utterance to refer to or be about something or to be true of a state of affairs? Or what it is for two people to speak the same language? Should a science of language completely eschew the need to explain meaning, understanding, reference, truth, languages, words, grammaticality, etc.? And, if called upon to defend this sense of what is "reasonable", might Dennett's "natives" not accuse the eliminativist of hypocrisy, asking him whether they are to conclude from his argument that his utterances don't mean anything, that he is not referring to or talking about anything when he speaks, that he is not speaking a language, that what he says is neither true nor false, and that he doesn't—indeed, could not possibly—even understand what he is being asked? And, if the eliminativist remained stoic in his reply, couldn't they drive their objection home by asking him why he doesn't go through his daily life acting as if he actually believes all those eliminativist claims?

On the other hand, if eliminating all the "fictions" from the *explananda* of a naturalistically reconceived science of language seems an unreasonable—indeed, a nonsensical and self-contradictory—option, what is the alternative? An alternative that has been adopted by many naturalist language scientists is to advocate only a limited eliminativism: that is, to seek ways to give naturalistic explanations of at least some folk-linguistic notions, while accepting that others, even most, are not legitimate *explananda* for the language sciences – that they are, in Dennett's phrase, members of a confused ontology. Not surprisingly, there is no consensus within naturalist language science regarding just which folk-linguistic notions should be treated as legitimate *explananda* (a.k.a. "linguistic facts") and which are not good theoretical entities ("folk-linguistic fictions"). However, these disagreements need not detain us here. For the challenge which must be faced regardless of any particular language scientist's choice of legitimate *explananda* from among the legacies of the Western linguistic tradition is how *any* can be incorporated within the naturalistic epistemology of a redefined language science: that is, to paraphrase Kitchener, without countenancing any non-naturalistic entities or properties, without attributing any non-naturalistic powers to acts of language or to language-users, and without employing any non-naturalistic methods. The generalized version of this challenge might be given the title of "The Hard Problem of Language", in analogy to Chalmers (1995) "Hard Problem of Consciousness" and Hutto and Myin's (2013) "Hard Problem of Content": How can a naturalized science which has made such progress in explaining basic, pre- and non-linguistic cognitive phenomena, "scale-up" to explain more sophisticated, "higher-level" cognitive processes and phenomena, particularly those concerning language?[2]

My goal in this paper is to suggest a way of addressing—indeed, of defeating—this challenge by means of reflecting on the everyday cultural practices of metalinguistic discourse.

---

[2] Cf. for some recent articles addressing these issues: Harvey (2015), Cuffari, Di Paolo, and De Jaegher (2014), Cowley (2011), Steffensen (2015), Rączaszek-Leonardi (2012), Thibault (2011), Cowley and Nash (2013). See also Maturana (1978).

3. Folk metalinguistic practices

In this Section I will merely give a summary of some of the most important and general conclusions that can be drawn from the last few decades' studies of folk metalinguistic practices. This summary draws on my own research as well as on that of anthropologists, developmental and social psychologists, descriptive linguists, rhetoricians, communication theorists, ethnomethodologists, discourse and conversation analysts, and sociolinguists.[3] The most detailed and explicitly theorized study of folk metalinguistic (or "folk reflexive") practices is to be found in Asif Agha's excellent *Language and Social Relations* (2007).

But first, consider the following examples of everyday metalinguistic remarks:

"That's what she said"
"What did he mean by that, anyway?"
"I'm talking about the one on the left"
"Sorry, could you say that again?"
"Did she understand what you said?"
"What does comely mean?"
"That's not true!"
"Yes, that's right."
"Why did he say that?"
"Will you explain that?"
"What's that called?"
"Is this what you're referring to?"
"I'll try to describe it to you."

---

[3] A selection of these is given in the references: Stross (1974), Silverstein (1985), Agar (1994), Silverstein and Urban (1996), Lucy (1993), Hanks (1993), Parmentier (1993), Hickmann (1993), Briggs (1993), Besnier (1993), Wolf et al. (1996), Bublitz and Huber (2007), Jaworski, Coupland, and Galasinski (2004), Davis (2001), Hyland (2005), French (2010), Rumsey (1990, 2013), Danziger (2013), Danziger and Rumsey (2013), Nevins and Nevins (2013), Odango (2016).

"I don't agree with that remark."
"What's his name?"
"No, soporific doesn't mean childish"
"[ikanamıks] and [ɛkanamıks] are the same word"
"I'm only teasing"
"Do you understand?"
"That's not what I told you to do"
"Please don't lie to me."
"Promise me you won't go."
"He said he was sorry."
"She ordered me to leave."
"I believe you"
"Really?"
"I'm glad to hear it."
"Would you ask him to shut up?"

  Remarks like these occur as a regular feature of mundane conversational exchanges between English speakers. Yet such remarks are only the most quotable tips of discourse-interactional icebergs. What is at issue in this paper are the everyday discursive practices (conversational routines, language-games) in which such metalinguistic remarks occur, and are often responded to, and in which some aspect of language or language activity is (to use the Anglophone metalinguistic expression) "talked about": referred to or appealed to, characterized, queried, commented on, objected to, defended, explained, made fun of, endorsed, sanctioned, described, and so on. Some additional examples of Anglophone folk metalinguistic practices are mentioned in Section 4 below.

  Research in an increasingly wide range of language com-munities around the world indicates the following about metalinguistic practices.

(i) Metalinguistic practices are pervasive and universal: a prevalent feature of daily life in every language, every culture.

(ii) Although every language culture has and makes common use of metalinguistic practices, ethnographers have given abundant evidence of their diversity in forms of expression, meanings and discursive functions, and in cultural patterns of use. Metalinguistic practices vary non-isomorphically along many different dimensions and exhibit the same kinds and breadth of cultural diversity as do other linguistic-cultural practices across and within speech communities worldwide. Agha refers to this diversity as a "central and inescapable fact about human societies… at any given time" (Agha, 2007, p. 1)

(iii) Metalinguistic practices address an almost limitless range of linguistic referents, with those familiar to a speaker of English (e.g., 'languages', 'names', 'meanings', 'descriptions', 'promises', 'implication', etc.) having no privileged or universal status, despite the assumptions underlying the Western linguistic tradition. Becoming competent in another culture's metalinguistic practices—especially a culture that has escaped the influence of the ideological behemoth that is Western metalinguistics—induces a similar experience of *depaysement* to that of becoming competent in its kinship systems, religious practices, social etiquette, plant taxonomies, folk psychologies, etc.

(iv) Like all discursive practices, metalinguistic practices are multifunctional, exhibiting a diverse and contextually-shifting range of interactional purposes and uses, from the shaping of particular discursive events (such as the exchange of introductions between strangers, a prayer meeting, a public lecture, a business meeting, a court trial, a romantic date, gossiping, etc.) to the management of such matters as social relations, personal and cultural identities, classroom interaction, cooperative undertakings, institutional processes, etc.

(v) Metalinguistic practices often have no uniquely identifying features, such as the use of particular sounds, words, formal patterns, etc. They are not separated off from, external to, or of a different logical order from other discursive activities. Like most of a culture's discursive practices or language-games, metalinguistic practices are "a motley, an open-ended, overlapping array which do not fit together as parts of a singly systematically related totality" (Williams, 2010). As Agha points out: "The use of metalinguistic words and expressions is but a tiny fragment of the range of native metalinguistic practices which the ethnographer observes (...) and all such devices have other uses as well." (Agha, 2007, p. 18-19)

(vi) Metalinguistic activity "calls little attention to itself, despite its ubiquity" (Agha, 2007, p. 20). Speakers and hearers are often not aware of the metalinguistic character of such activities and may find it difficult to bring this to conscious awareness when questioned by ethnographers (Silverstein, 1981). Agha quotes Roman Jakobson (1960): "Like Moliere's Jourdain who used prose without knowing it, we practice metalanguage without realizing the metalingual character of our operations" (Agha, 2007, p. 18)

(vii) Like all discursive practices, metalinguistic practices are normative: that is, one's participation in metalinguistic practices—how one produces or responds to a metalinguistic remark—is the subject of normative attention and reflexive regulation (Heritage, 1984; Taylor, 1997).

(viii) An essential component of the child's developing linguistic abilities and emerging membership of her linguistic community is her increasingly competent participation in metalinguistic practices, first in how she responds to the metalinguistic remarks of others and, as time progresses, in the production of metalinguistically-oriented remarks of her own

(Hickmann, 1993; Taylor, 2012, 2013; Taylor & van den Herik, 2021; Watson-Gegeo & Gegeo, 1986).

4. A thought-experiment

In discussing the character and function of folk metalinguistic practices it is instructive to consider what language and language activities would be like without them. Imagine a Twin Earth which has the following characteristics: the only language spoken on Twin Earth is identical with English as spoken on Earth, except that there are no means for engaging in metalinguistic discourse. So, although Twin-Earthlings produce words and utterances that sound exactly like the English words and sentences produced on Earth and although they appear to understand these words and sentences as English-speaking Earthlings do, nonetheless, Twin-Earthlings have no way of making the kind of metalinguistic remarks that are listed at the beginning of Section 3.

Shorn of these kinds of metalinguistic tools, a Twin-Earthling cannot engage in metalinguistic practices such as explaining to someone what he is referring to or talking about. Nor can he ask someone else what they are referring to or talking about. That is, he cannot ask questions like "Which of them are you referring to?" or declare "I'm talking about that one, not the one over there". He cannot request another Twin-Earthling to explain what she meant (by what she just said) or describe what he had understood her to mean. That is, a Twin-Earthling cannot *do* what we metalinguistically-endowed Earthlings in appropriate circumstances would *call* "explaining what I am referring to", "saying what I am asking about", "explaining what I meant", or "saying what I understood". Nor can he claim—or deny—to be talking about the same thing (or event or idea, etc.) that someone else is talking about. And he cannot say what a particular expression means; he cannot even refer to it, nor, having spoken again, can he describe this as "repeating" or "saying again" what he said before.

On a Twin Earth devoid of metalinguistic practices, a speaker cannot deny or affirm the truth of what somebody says, or explain why it is true (or false). She cannot even state that she agrees or disagrees with what that person said. She cannot assert or deny that what you are doing is what she asked you to do—or that it is or isn't what you said you would do—and she cannot explain why that is so. She cannot characterize something she (or someone else) says as a promise, or as a threat, or as a prediction, or as a mistake, or as a lie, or as an order, or as her name. She is unable to claim that she understands (or does not understand) what someone just said; nor can she explain her reasons for that claim. She does not have the means to say whether what transpires is or isn't the same as what she (or someone else) said would happen. And she cannot claim that what you just said does or doesn't make sense or follow from, or conflict with, what you (or someone else) said before.

A Twin-Earthling cannot speak of a part of an utterance as a word – or speak of its meaning. She cannot even characterize what she just did as "saying" something. Nor can she speak of names (of places, people, etc.) or of languages – or, indeed, of language. She cannot assert that what someone says, or what she herself says, is correct or incorrect, is right or wrong, or is true or false. She cannot claim that how things actually are is or isn't in accord with the way that they were said to be. And so, naturally, there can be no disagreements over such claims.

A Twin-Earthling parent cannot explain what he says to a child or correct the child's statement or use of a word, or make any other sort of comment about her linguistic behavior. He cannot ask what her name is. Nor can he explain to the child (or anyone else) that a particular utterance means you should or shouldn't do such-and-such or evaluate whether what she actually does is or isn't what she was told to do. And no Twin-Earthling can read or write, because the practices by which one learns these activities must necessarily involve metalinguistic discourse.

Within language theory, the received view of folk metalinguistic practices is that they are epiphenomenal – trivial and supplementary add-ons to the real business of language: something like customized user-friendly-interfaces with which different cultures over-lay the underlying linguistic operating system. However, what I believe this thought experiment shows is that being a competent speaker of Twin-Earthling English would be fundamentally—indeed, categorically—different from being a competent speaker of Earthling English. Indeed, it suggests that <u>all</u> language activities on a metalinguistically-deprived Twin Earth would be immeasurably different from—could be nothing like—Anglophone language activities on Earth: that is, if a Twin-Earthling could do none of these 'things' that we Earthling Anglophones do in metalinguistic exchanges. To put this claim in positive terms: Anglophone language practices can only be what they are—that is, what we Anglophones know and *count on* them to be, moment by moment, through every living day—because being a competent Anglophone necessarily includes being a competent participant in Anglophone metalinguistic practices. And, naturally, this positive claim applies *mutatis mutandis* to all forms of human languaging—i.e., to all 'languages'—which makes the fact, as was noted above, that metalinguistic terms and practices vary widely and in unexpected ways among Earth's thousands of diverse linguistic communities infinitely more important to the study of language than is suggested by the metaphor of user-friendly cultural interfaces overlaying "the real business" of language. On the contrary, *it is because of metalinguistic practices that the real business of language can take place at all.*

To go one step further, it is worth asking how, shorn of metalinguistic practices, it would be possible for the cultural life of Twin-Earthlings to be anything like *cultural forms of life* on Earth. For instance, if it were not possible to speak met-alinguis-tically of two utterances as meaning the same, or as not meaning the same, or of one of them as true or false, then how could two people have an argument, or cooperate in performing a complex task or solving a problem, or get married, or play games, or translate from another language, or make and enforce laws, or explain or object to someone's reasoning, or teach a child, or make and test predictions, or worship supernatural beings, or plan for the future? If it were not possible to affirm or deny that what someone is doing is the same as what we "told them to do", or is or isn't "what we agreed"—and to hold such characterizations normatively accountable—then how could the verbal-uttering part of language connect up with the 'doing' part? How could a kind of language shorn of metalinguistic practices possibly serve our human forms of living and doing and thinking and interacting in the countless ways, moment-to-moment, which we depend on language for? It would seem, I suggest, that we need metalinguistic practices not only in order for language to be the kind of thing we depend on language to be, but also in order for the forms of life we live and act and think in to exist at all.

5. Conclusions

What conclusions might we then draw for the language sciences and the Hard Problem of Language?

1. Instead of peripheralizing them, the sciences of language must move to the very center of their investigatory domain the folk metalinguistic practices by means of which 'we' (the

various genera of 'folk') are constantly making and re-making language what it is for 'us', in our widely varying ways in cultural communities around the world, and, no less importantly, the means by which we make language what it is for 'us' *as humans*.

2. However, language science must resist the powerful inclination to reductively misrepresent such metalinguistic practices: in particular, by attributing the essential roles that they have in our forms of language and life as stemming from their purportedly propositional character. It is by these reductive means that are generated the folk-linguistic fictions that make up the furniture of the Western linguistic imaginary: that is, by decontextualizing customary utterances made in the course of folk metalinguistic practices—and the commonplace generalizations derived from such utterances—and recontextualizing them within the intellectual practices of empirical justification.[4] In other words, mundane metalinguistic utterances such as "My name is 'Margaret'" and "She is talking about her mother"—or the generalizations "*Comely* means 'pleasing to look at'" and "[ikanamıks] is the same word as [ɛkanamıks]"—are removed from their everyday interactional contexts and represented as empirical propositions. As such, they are treated as uniquely evaluable as true or false depending on whether the states of affairs they are taken to assert do in fact obtain: that is, whether the speaker's name *actually is* "Margaret", whether the speaker referred to *is in fact* talking about her mother, whether the word *comely really does* mean 'pleasing to look at', and whether [ikanamıks] *truly is* the same word as [ɛkanamıks]. Accordingly, taking any such utterance as true—for whatever reason—thus seems to presuppose a first-order *linguistic fact* requiring explanation: e.g., the

---

[4] This rhetorical process of "theorizing language" is the topic of Taylor (1992, 1997).

metalanguage-independent fact that "Margaret" is the speaker's name or that *comely* means 'pleasing to look at'. Yet a naturalistically-inclined language scientist should ask: What is the ontology of such facts? How is the naturalist to give such *explananda* an epistemologically satisfactory explanation: that is, to repeat Kitchener, "without countenancing any non-naturalistic entities or properties, without attributing any non-naturalistic powers to acts of language or to language-users, and without employing any non-naturalistic methods"? It is in the theorizing misrepresentation of the role of the commonplace remarks made within folk metalinguistic practices that we find the source of the Western linguistic imaginary, its reified "fictions", and the resultant Hard Problem of Language.

3. A redefined language science would do well to accept as a fundamental principle that, *within a culture's folk metalinguistic practices*, issues concerning such things as word- and sentence-meanings, word-identity, languages, reference, understanding, correctness, etc. already have all the explanations which, in practice, they ever require. These are explanations that are *enacted and made to matter* (in the only ways that they do matter) within the moment-to-moment, culturally-diverse, context-dependent, interactionally negotiated, and embodied practices of everyday metalinguistic discourse. While there is clearly much to research and explain in the sciences of language for which a naturalistic approach is most appropriately suited, the real challenge is to resist the temptation to present the results of such research as natural-science explanations of the reified fictions of the Western linguistic imaginary.

References
Agar, M. (1994). *Language shock: Understanding the culture of conversation*. New York: William Morrow.

Agha, A. (2007). *Language and social relations*. Cambridge: Cambridge University Press.

Auroux, S. (1989). *Histoire des idées linguistiques: La naissance des metalangues en Orient et en Occident*. Liege: Pierre Mardaga.

Baumann, R., & Briggs, C. (2003). *Voices of modernity: Language ideologies and the politics of inequality*. Cambridge UK: Cambridge University Press.

Besnier, N. (1993). Reported speech and affect on Nukulaelae atoll. In J. Hill, & J. Irvine (Eds.), *Responsibility and evidence in oral discourse*. Cambridge: Cambridge University Press.

Braddon-Mitchell, D., & Nola, R. (Eds.). (2009). *Conceptual analysis and philosophical naturalism*. Cambridge: Cambridge University Press.

Briggs, C. (1993). Generic versus metapragmatic dimensions of Warao narratives: who regiments performance? In J. Lucy (Ed.), *Reflexive language: Reported speech and metapragmatics*. Cambridge UK: Cambridge University Press.

Bublitiz, W., & Hubler, A. (Eds.). (2007). *Metapragmatics in use*. Amsterdam: John Benjamins.

Chalmers, D. J. (1995). Facing up to the problem of consciousness. *Journal of Consciousness Studies*, 2, 200-219.

Churchland, P. (1991). Folk psychology and the explanation of human behavior. In J. D. Greenwood (Ed.), *The future of folk psychology*. Cambridge: Cambridge University Press.

Churchland, P. (2007). The evolving fortunes of eliminativist materialism. In B. McLaughlin, & J. Cohen (Eds.), *Contemporary debates in philosophy of mind*. Oxford: Blackwell Publishing.

Cowley, S. (2011). Taking a language stance. *Ecological Psychology*, 23, 1-25.

Cowley, S., & Nash, L. (2013). Language, interactivity, and solution probing: repetition without repetition. *Adaptive Behavior*, 21, 187-198.

Cuffari, E., Di Paolo, E., & De Jaegher, H. (2014). From participatory sensemaking to language : there and back again. *Phenomenology and the Cognitive Sciences*, 14.

Danziger, E. (2013). Conventional wisdom: imagination, obedience and intersubjectivity. *Language & Communication*, 33(3).

Danziger, E., & Rumsey, A. (2013). From opacity to intersubjectivity across languages and cultures. *Language & Communication*, 33(3).

Davis, H. (2001). *Words: An integrational approach.* London: Routledge.

Demuth, K. (1986). Prompting routines in the language socialization of Basotho children. In B. Schieffelin, & E. Ochs (Eds.), *Language socialization across cultures*. Cambridge: Cambridge University Press.

Dennett, D. (1981). *Brainstorms.* Cambridge MA: MIT Press.

French, B. (2010). *Maya ethnolinguistic identity*. Tucson: University of Arizona Press.

Greenwood, J. (Ed.). (1991). *The future of folk psychology*. Cambridge: Cambridge University Press.

Hanks, W. (1993). Metalanguage and pragmatics of deixis. In J. Lucy (Ed.), *Reflexive language: Reported speech and metapragmatics*. Cambridge: Cambridge University Press.

Harris, R. (1980). *The language-maker*. London: Duckworth.

Harris, R. (1981). *The language myth*. London: Duckworth.

Harris, R. (1987). *The language machine*. London: Duckworth.

Harris, R., & Taylor, T. J. (1997). *Landmarks in linguistic thought: The western tradition from Socrates to Saussure*. London: Routledge.

Harvey, M. (2015). Content in languaging: enaction and anti-representationalism. *Language Sciences*, 90, 90-129.

Heritage, J. (1984). *Garfinkel and ethnomethodology*. Cambridge, UK: Polity Press.

Hickmann, M. (1993). The boundaries of reported speech in narrative discourse: some developmental aspects. In J. Lucy (Ed.), *Reflexive language: Reported speech and metapragmatics*. Cambridge: Cambridge University Press.

Hutto, D. (2011). Presumptuous naturalism. *American Philosophical Quarterly*, 48(2), 129-145.

Hutto, D., & Myin, E. (2013). *Radicalizing enactivism: Basic minds without content*. Cambridge MA: MIT Press.

Hyland, K. (2005). *Metadiscourse*. London: Continuum.

Jakobson, R. (1960). Closing statement: linguistic poetics. In T. Sebeok (Ed.), *Style in language*. Cambridge MA: MIT Press.

Jaworski, A., Coupland, N., & Galasinski, D. (Eds.). (2004). *Metalanguage: Social and ideological perspectives*. Berlin and New York: Mouton de Gruyter.

Kitchener, R. F. (2006). Genetic epistemology: Naturalistic epistemology vs. normative epistemology. In L. Smith, & J. Vonèche (Eds.), *Norms in human development*. Cambridge, U.K: Cambridge University Press.

Linell, P. (2005). *The written language bias in linguistics*. London: Routledge.

Love, N. (2004). Cognition and the language myth. *Language Sciences*, 26, 525-544.

Lucy, J. (1993). Metapragmatic presentationals: reporting speech with quotatives in Yucatec Maya. In J. Lucy (Ed.), *Reflexive language: Reported speech and metapragmatics*. Cambridge: Cambridge University Press.

Maturana, H. (1978). Biology of language: the epistemology of reality. In G. Miller, & E. Lenneberg (Eds.), *Psychology and biology of language and thought: Essays in honor of Eric Lenneberg*. New York: Academic Press.

Nevins, T., & Nevins, E. (2013). Speaking in the mirror of the other: dialectics of intersubjectivity and temporality in Western Apache discourse. *Language & Communication*, 33(3).

Odango, E. (2016). A discourse-based approach to the language documentation of local ecological knowledge. *Language Documentation & Conservation* 10, 107-154.

Parmentier, R. (1993). The political function of reported speech: a Belauan example. In J. Lucy (Ed.), *Reflexive language: Reported speech and metapragmatics*. Cambridge UK: Cambridge University Press.

Rączaszek-Leonardi, J. (2012). Language as a system of replicable constraints. In *Laws, language and life: Howard Pattee's classic papers on the physics of symbols*. Springer.

Reddy, M. J. (1979). The conduit metaphor: a case of frame conflict in our language about language. In A. Ortony (Ed.), *Metaphor and thought*. Cambridge: Cambridge University Press.

Rumsey, A. (2013). Intersubjectivity, deception and the 'opacity of other minds': perspectives from highland New Guinea and beyond. *Language & Communication*, 33(3).

Rumsey, A. (1990). Wording, meaning, and linguistic ideology. *American Anthropologist*, 92.

Silverstein, M. (1981). The limits of awareness. In *Sociolinguistic Working Papers*, no.84. Austin TX: Southwest Educational Development Laboratory.

Silverstein, M. (1985). The culture of language in Chinookan narrative texts: or, on saying that... in Chinook. In J. Nichols, & A. Woodbury (Eds.), *Grammar inside and outside the clause*. Cambridge: Cambridge University Press.

Silverstein, M., & Urban, G. (Eds.). (1996). *Natural histories of discourse*. Chicago: Chicago University Press.

Steffensen, S. (2015). Distributed language and dialogism: notes on non-locality, sense-making, and interactivity. *Language Sciences*, 30, 1-15.

Stitch, S. (1996). *From folk psychology to cognitive science: The case against belief*. Cambridge: MIT Press.

Stross, B. (1974). Speaking of speaking: Tenejapa Tzeltal metalinguistics. In *Explanations in the ethnography of speaking*. Cambridge: Cambridge University Press.

Taylor, T. J. (1992). *Mutual misunderstanding: Scepticism and the theorizing of language and interpretation*. Durham NC: Duke University Press.

Taylor, T. J. (1997). Enculturating language. In *Theorizing language: Analysis, normativity, rhetoric, history*. Oxford: Pergamon Press.

Taylor, T. J. (2012). Understanding others and understanding language: how do children do it? *Language Sciences*, 34, 1-12.

Taylor, T. J. (2013). Calibrating the child for language: Meredith Williams on a Wittgensteinian approach to language socialization. *Language Sciences*, 40, 308-320.

Taylor, T.J. and van den Herik (2021). Metalinguistic exchanges in child language development. *Language Sciences* 88(5): 101434

Thibault, P. J. (2011). First-order languaging dynamics and second-order language. *Ecological Psychology*, 23(3), 210-245.

Watson, J. (1924). *Behaviorism*. Chicago: University of Chicago Press.

Watson-Gegeo, K., & Gegeo, D. (1986). Calling-out and repeating routines in Kwara'ae children's language socialization. In B. Schieffelin, & E. Ochs (Eds.), *Language socialization across cultures*. Cambridge: Cambridge University Press.

Wheeler, M. (2005). *Reconstructing the cognitive world*. Cambridge: MIT Press.

Williams, M. (2010). *Blind obedience: Paradox and learning in the later Wittgenstein*. London: Routledge.

Wolf, G., Bocquillon, M., de la Houssaye, D., Krzyzek, P., Meynard, C., & Philip, L. (1996). Pronouncing French names in New Orleans. *Language in Society*, 25(3).

IV

Why we need a theory of language

The question to which the title of this paper alludes could also be expressed in the following way: Why have language theorists in the Western tradition acted as if they felt compelled to discuss, over and over again, what are apparently the same questions, the same controversies, the same arguments, the same theories, etc.? Another way of putting this: why do they feel a need to produce theories of language, as these latter are understood within the history of Western thought? The historian of linguistic ideas fashions an answer to this question by making use of the explanatory tools provided by such concepts as 'intellectual tradition', 'historical influence', and 'conceptual inheritance'. It is not my intention to argue against this way of addressing the question of continuity in Western linguistic thought, and for the very simple reason that I think it makes a great deal of sense. Nevertheless, it is my intention to approach that question from a different direction, to view it from an unfamiliar perspective, so as to make sense of it differently than it is made sense of from the perspective afforded by the history of ideas.

I will present a hypothetical account of what might be called 'the rhetorical source' of language theory. I will not argue for that account here: I will merely present it. My aim is to see if it can be made sense of. For if we find that it can be made sense of—that is, that the continuous threads uniting Western linguistic thought can intelligibly be represented as the product of otherwise unremarkable patterns of everyday discourse—that very realization will itself, I believe, make this a useful exercise.

The premise underlying this approach, in short, is this. In order to break free from the intellectual constraints of the Western linguistic tradition, it is not enough simply to chart the myth-ological features of that tradition, to uncover its logical and conceptual presuppositions, to chronicle its historical development, and to strive to solve its problems and correct its mistakes 'once and for all'. For it is we ourselves—in our non-professional identities as ordinary language-users—who unwittingly regenerate the source of that tradition and who exercise the authority by which continued submission to its constraints is enforced. The essential features of that tradition emerge whenever we are in those discursive circumstances which oblige us to speak or think 'seriously' about language: in informal arguments, in after-class conversations, in seminar discussions, etc. In other words, it is in these dialogic contexts—when we are called upon to *justify* what in other contexts would probably strike us as perfectly mundane, 'innocuous' metalinguistic remarks—that the 'synchronic' origin of the Western linguistic tradition may be found: an origin, that is, located not in Ancient Athens or seventeenth-century Europe but in what, if asked, we might simply call 'ordinary commonsense'. It is, therefore, here we must look to determine why we find that tradition's problems and arguments so compelling: to understand why they make sense to us and why we feel a need to address them. And it is perhaps by thus bringing ourselves to recognize the source of our compulsion to adhere to, and indeed to continue weaving, the Western linguistic myth, that we may find the means to free ourselves from its entanglement.

My strategy, therefore, will be to present an account of linguistic theorizing as a rhetorical derivative of what I will call 'the commonsense picture of language'. I will begin by explaining what I mean by 'the commonsense picture of language' and will then discuss how that picture can be seen as generating the puzzles that characterize the intellectual discourses of modern Western linguistic thought.

What do I mean by the commonsense picture of language? Well, nothing too controversial. It is hardly controversial to say:

1. That we usually understand what we say to each other.
2. That to understand someone's utterance, we must understand what it means.
3. That words have meanings.
4. That the meaning a sentence has in a given language is not a matter determined by the wishes of any single speaker or hearer, writer or reader.
5. That when we speak, we express our thoughts.
6. That by speaking we may refer to things.
7. That the truth or falsity of what we say depends on how the things we refer to really are.
8. That many of us know and use the same language.

Pretty clearly, only someone who would typically be called a 'sceptic' would want to *deny* these and other similar claims. That is, only such a sceptic would maintain:

1'. That we don't usually understand each other.
2'. That we don't have to understand the meaning of someone's utterance in order to understand that utterance.
3'. That words don't in fact mean anything at all.
4'. That a sentence means whatever anyone wants it to mean.
5'. That when we speak, we aren't expressing our thoughts.
6'. That our utterances never really refer to anything.
7'. That the truth or falsity of what we say is independent of how the things we refer to really are.
8'. That, surprising though it may seem, there are no two people who speak the same language.

Indeed, the fact that someone who denied claims like 1-8 would be treated as a sceptic is directly related (as two sides of the same coin) to our readiness to characterize those claims as what we call 'commonsense'. Accordingly, we will probably treat the sceptic's denial of such claims as controversial and dismiss his position as 'an assault on commonsense'. And this holds regardless of whether we are dealing with a 'strong' sceptic, who denies the truth of 1-8, or with a 'weak' sceptic, who merely denies that we are justified in taking their truth for granted.

It goes without saying that part and parcel of taking claims like 1-8 *to be commonsense* is taking them to be *true*. (Thus another word for a statement of 'commonsense' is 'truism'.) Moreover, just as commonsense tells us (see no. 7 above) that the only reason the sentence 'Mars has two moons' is true is that there *really are* two of the things we call 'moons' revolving around the planet we call 'Mars', we also take the truth of the claims 1-8 to inhere in the fact that things really are as those claims state them to be: that is, we take them to be true *because* they correspond to the facts.

Take no. 3 as an example: 'Words have meanings.' That sentence is assumed to be true *because* the words we use *really do* have meanings. This is just another way of saying that if, in fact, the words we use *did not* really have any meanings, then no. 3 would be *false*. Therefore, the sentence 'Words have meanings' is not just some groundless platitude or meaningless tautology that we mouth dogmatically to each other; it actually corresponds to 'the real facts' about words, facts that are independent of our awareness of them or of how we describe them. Commonsense tells us that we don't *just say* that words have meanings; *they really do*. And, by extension, the same goes for the other statements listed in 1-8 above and for other similarly commonsense truisms about language and communication.

What this comes down to is that 'commonsense'—of which the eight claims above are intended as representative samples—provides a very rich and complex picture of the communicational reality (the 'facts') *underlying* ordinary communicational behavior. We may not be able directly to observe components of that reality: such as the meanings of words, or the English language, or states of mutual understanding. But no matter, for 'commonsense' confirms that there definitely is a reality there for us to study, to describe, and to explain: in short, to theorize. It is in this way that language theory acquires its investigative assignment.

To see this, consider the example of no. 1. When treated as an empirical truth, the claim that 'We usually understand what we say to each other' naturally leads to a host of very puzzling questions. For instance, what particular kinds of facts must obtain for two communicators to understand what they say to each other? Can we determine what these facts are? Are they facts about the communicator's mental states, about their brains, about their bodies, about the contextual circumstances, about their observable behavior, about the behavior of their co-interactants, about the social structure of their community, etc.? And, whatever these facts are determined to be, how can we explain their occurrence? In other words, if we can presume that communicators ordinarily *do* understand each other and that mutual understanding consists in some determinate state of affairs, what explanation can we give for the obtaining of that state of affairs: *how* do communicators come to understand (thus conceived) what they say to each other?

Questions such as these are the very stuff of the intellectual discourse that is language theory. Accordingly, the goal of the theorist of language is to provide answers to such questions, the puzzling nature of which is a legacy of the *a priori* status which is accorded to some or all of the claims that make up the commonsense picture of language. It is the theorist's attempts to answer these questions that act as the continuous threads running through the length of Western linguistic thought, weaving it into a single discursive fabric. Consequently, the fact that language theories in the Western tradition have again and again encountered the same puzzles, have applied to them the same strategies, and have come up with the same 'solutions' should be the cause of no particular surprise. For the discursive continuity of Western linguistic thought can be seen as the inevitable legacy of its rhetorical origins: that is, of the interpretation of commonsense claims about language and communication as empirical truths.

Within this discourse, the task assigned to language theory is

(a) to describe, in as much detail and as accurately as possible, the underlying reality—the facts—that the commonsense picture of language and communication is true *of*, and
(b) to explain how those facts occur.

Let me illustrate this with some cases from the history of Western linguistic thought, taking the theoretical treatment of claim no. 1 as my particular example: 'We usually understand what we say to each other.' (For a much fuller discussion of these examples, cf. Taylor, 1992.)

In the European Enlightenment, we find language theorists describing communicational understanding in terms of the qualitative identity of mental content. That is, it is held to be true that I understand what you say if and only if the following state of affairs obtains: your utterance produces ideas in my mind that are qualitatively identical to those ideas in your mind which your utterance was intended to express. This conception of communicational understanding is clearly articulated in the following passage from Locke's *Essay*.

> To make words serviceable to the end of communication, it is necessary that they excite in the hearer exactly the same idea that they stand for in the mind of the speaker. Without this, men fill one another's heads with noise and sounds; but convey not thereby their thoughts, and lay not before one another their ideas, which is the end of discourse and language (Locke, 1690, III, ix, 6).

But how can such a state of affairs come to obtain? That is, how can your words produce the same ideas in my mind that you intended to express by uttering those words? Addressing this question, the French philosopher Condillac, a self-declared follower of Locke, argued that language could *not* in fact be a vehicle of communicational understanding, thus conceived, UNLESS the connections between words and ideas were somehow given in nature. Only the shared natural history of human communicators could possibly provide the intersubjective bond required to explain their mutual understanding of words. Thus, in the following passages, Condillac suggests that a language based not on natural principles, but on arbitrary choices, could never be a successful vehicle of communicational understanding:

> It is a mistake to think that in the first creation of languages men could choose indifferently and arbitrarily which words were to be the signs of which ideas. If this had been the case, how could they have understood one another? (Condillac, 1947, 365-366). Nature, which is the beginning of everything, begins articulate language... and analogy, which completes the task, does it well to the extent that it continues in the way that nature began (Condillac, 1981, 2).

In other words, Condillac's reasoning proceeds as follows.

> Premise 1: Since we know, as commonsense assures, that communicators usually *do* understand each other, and
>
> Premise 2: since we know, following Locke, that understanding requires qualitative identity of mental content, and
>
> Premise 3: since a language which is not based on natural principles could not be a vehicle of communicational understanding, thus defined,
>
> Conclusion, we may therefore be certain that the connections between words and ideas in a language are in fact based on natural principles.

On the other hand, the founder of linguistic structuralism, Ferdinand de Saussure, reasoned that communicational understanding must consist not—as Enlightenment theorists had supposed—in the qualitative identity of the speaker and hearer's mental content, but in its *formal* identity. For two people to understand each other it must be that the concept (signified) which each associates with a given signifier has the same formal value, which is determined solely by that concept's structural place in the system of differential relations that is a language (*langue*). In other words, for you and I to understand what we say to each other we must both have internalized and must both be using the same *langue*, conceived as a structured system of differential relations between arbitrary signs. Without the use of such a mutually internalized language system, Saussure argues, it would be impossible for us to share the same concepts and signifiers, and, therefore, also impossible for our acts of speech to result in communicational understanding. 'A language is necessary in order that speech should be intelligible' (Saussure, 1916, 37). Consequently, *since we can take for granted the commonsense claim that communicational understanding is a perfectly ordinary occurrence*, we can conclude with confidence that such internalized language systems really do exist. In other words, it is not by empirical observation that Saussure comes to the conclusion cited in the following passage; it is forced upon him by his assumption that whatever kind of entity a language is, it *must* be something that makes communicational understanding possible. (For if it were not, then communicational understanding would not be possible; *and yet we know it is!*)

> A language is a method, an instrument, perfectly suited to accomplish constantly and immediately its purpose: to make oneself understood (Saussure, 1974, 16).

Writing at about the same time, the German philosopher Gottlob Frege made use of a different possible 'solution' to the same rhetorical puzzle. Frege argued that if it were true that communicational understanding required identity of speaker and hearer's mental content, then it would be *impossible* for any speaker and hearer ever to understand each other.

> It is so much of the essence of any one of my ideas to be a content of my consciousness, that any idea someone else has is, just as such, different from mine (Frege, 1984, 361).

Consequently, *since we know that speakers and hearers <u>do</u> usually understand each other*, Frege continues, we may conclude that communicational understanding consists in something other than identity of mental content. Instead, Frege reminds us of the commonsense truism (cf. no. 2 above) that if you understand my words, then you understand what those words mean. In other words, our mutual understanding consists in our common grasp of the *same thing*: namely, the meanings of the words used. That is, for communicational understanding to be possible at all, our understanding of a word cannot involve *two* things: your mental meaning (or idea) and mine. Rather, it must be the case that every word has an objective, person-independent, non-mental meaning and that this objective meaning (or sense) is graspable by you and me as the very same thing. Our mutual understanding of that word will thus consist in our shared grasp of its objective meaning. Such an objective meaning

> is not the result of an inner process or the product of a mental act which men perform, but something objective: that is to say, it is something that is exactly the same for all rational beings, for all who are capable of

grasping it, just as the Sun, say, is something objective (Frege, 1979, 7).

Again, what interests me in Frege's theory is not this conclusion, but the rhetoric of the argument by which that conclusion is motivated. It has the following structure.

Premise 1: We do usually understand each other.

Premise 2: For two people to understand each other, each must grasp the same thing: namely, the meanings of the speaker's words.

Premise 3: If the meanings of words were something mental, then it would not be possible for two people, in grasping the meaning of a word, to grasp the same thing.

Conclusion: Words must therefore have objective meanings, independent of the mental content associated to them by individual communicators.

Note that, given the commonsense character of the premises (1) and (2), Frege's conclusion accrues an almost irresistible rhetorical force.

Pragmatic theorists, such as Dan Sperber and Deirdre Wilson (cf. Sperber and Wilson, 1986), take communicational understanding to consist not in the matching of mental content or in a mutual grasp of an objective sense but in the speaker and hearer pursuing a 'similar train of thought'. That is, the speaker and hearer must draw similar inferences from what is said, and similarly see the relevance of what is said to the interactional context in which it is said. But how could this occur? Sperber and Wilson maintain that communicational understanding would be impossible if speakers and hearers were *not* naturally equipped with the same inference-drawing mechanisms. If the drawing of pragmatic inferences were an arbitrary process under the communicator's voluntary control, what could possibly lead them to draw the same inferences and agree on the relevance of the speaker's utterance to the interactional context? That is, how could they possibly come to understand each other? Therefore, given (a) Sperber and Wilson's view of the nature of communicational understanding and (b) given the commonsense truism that communicational understanding does regularly occur, we are led ineluctably to the conclusion that speakers *do* naturally follow the same inference-drawing procedures, governed by what Sperber and Wilson call the 'Principle of Relevance'.

> Our claim is that all human beings automatically aim at the most efficient information processing possible. This is so whether they are conscious of it or not (Sperber and Wilson, 1986, 49).

> Communicators do not 'follow' the principle of relevance; and they could not violate it even if they wanted to. The principle of relevance applies without exception (Sperber and Wilson, 1986, 162).

The last account of understanding that I will mention here is that of the conversation analysts of the ethnomethodological school, such as Emmanuel Schegloff and John Heritage. What is distinctive about the ethnomethodological account of communicational understanding is that it does not take understanding to consist in shared mental contents, in the mutual grasping of objective meanings, or in similar psychological inferencing procedures. If that were what communicational understanding consisted in, the ethnomethodologist maintains, then it would be impossible. But of course communicational understanding does occur. Our 'commonsense' view of the world is clear on this: we *do* usually understand each other. Therefore, communicational understanding must consist in something *other than* what Condillac, Saussure, Frege, Sperber, and Wilson have assumed it to consist in. It cannot consist in a private mental state or process or in the mutual grasping of mysterious Platonic entities. It must, the ethnomethodologist argues, consist instead in something the obtaining of which we can confirm without the need of postulating such theoretical phantasms. Communicational understanding must consist in something straightforwardly observable in the public practice of verbal interaction.

The ethnomethodologist thus concludes that we need look no further in identifying instances of communicational understanding than the observable characteristics of those particular interactional events that communicators themselves count as instances of mutual understanding. In other words, for the ethnomethodologist, if two communicators treat their interactional events as instances of mutual understanding—at the very least by *not* treating them as instances of *misunderstanding*—then those interactional events are instances of mutual understanding. Whatever actual communicators accept as instances of mutual understanding, *that* is what communicational understanding is. In this case the theorist is wrong to treat the observable characteristics of communicational events as *evidence* of 'the real thing'—i.e. understanding itself—and he is confused if he thinks he must look in the communicator's minds or in Platonic heaven in order to find true understanding. Rather, whatever actual communicators, in particular communicational circumstances accept as instances of mutual understanding, *that* is what communicational understanding is. It has been right there before our eyes all the time. (Indeed, the ethnomethodologist argues, how could it not have been? If mutual understanding had really been something unobservable—in hidden Platonic or psychological realms—how could two people ever have known if they understood each other? And yet, of course, we know that communicators usually do understand each other.) What the language theorist should, therefore, do is *describe* the observable features of communicational interaction; for, in so doing, he will be giving an account of what it is for two people to understand each other.

> Rather than treating intersubjectivity as an essentially philosophical problem for which a determinate in-principle solution must be found, [the ethnomethodologist] treats its achievement and maintenance as a *practical* 'problem' which is routinely 'solved' by social actors in the course of their dealings with one another (Heritage, 1984, 54).

What I hope emerges from this quick sketch is that while each theory takes the regular achievement of communicational understanding for granted, they also each take that achievement to *consist* in something different. What is, therefore, essential in the discursive construction of a theory of communicational understanding is the presupposition of the truth of the claim *that it ordinarily occurs*. It is left up to the theorist to determine WHAT state of affairs that claim is true of.

In other words, THAT we do usually understand each other is invariably treated as a synthetic, *a priori* truth; WHAT it is for us to understand each other, and HOW its occurrence may be explained, these are matters for theoretical determination. In general, then, the rhetorical legacy of the commonsense picture of language and communication is limited to the presumed *truth* of remarks like 1-8. The task assigned to the language theorist is, therefore, one of solving the resultant discursive puzzles for the empty variables WHAT and HOW.

If this somewhat depressing account of the rhetorical origins and legacy of language theory makes any sense, then it will naturally focus our attention on the following question. Why must theorizing about language begin by presuming the truth of commonsense claims such as those listed 1-8? Why don't language theorists, like their colleagues in the natural sciences, adopt a more sceptical attitude toward whatever it is that 'commonsense' tells them about their chosen subject? Or, to come at it from a different angle, *why do I assume* that no one would ever reject the commonsense picture of language and communication, at least not its basic outlines? What are the grounds for *this* assumption? My answer, in short, is that if we gave into a wholesale sceptical rejection of that picture, we would be unable to live.

We accord propositions such as 1-8 the status of commonsense truisms because we take them to be nothing more than generalized formulations of the countless trivial, circumstance-specific remarks we regularly make about communicational events. (Analogously, 'Molly usually wears a red dress on Friday' is a generalized formulation of countless specific remarks of the type 'Molly wore a red dress on Friday.') In other words, we take propositions such as 1-8 to be generalized formulations of (what I will call) commonplace '*metadiscursive*' remarks. (By 'metadiscursive', I mean here discourse which reflexively concerns—which 'reflects back on'—discursive behavior itself: in other words, *talk about talk*.) The following are typical examples of metadiscourse.

9. 'OK , we understand each other then.'
10. 'Sure, I understand the meaning of your remark.'
11. 'Guess what? I just learned what soporific means.'
12. 'No, you nitwit; soporific doesn't mean "fatally poisonous"; what it really means is "sleep-inducing"'.
13. 'My letter clearly expresses my thoughts on the matter.'

14. 'Well, what I was referring to was his sarcastic tone, not what he actually said.'
15. 'Look, he's not actually in his room, so the fact of the matter is that what you said is false.'
16. 'If we hadn't all spoken the same language, our meeting would have been even more of a disaster.'

I take it that metadiscursive remarks such as these are a common and familiar feature of our daily lives. Now, imagine someone who went about claiming all instances of such ordinary metadiscursive remarks to be falsehoods. In other words, they claim it to be untrue whenever anyone says of themselves, or of anyone else,

> that they understood what someone else said ('No, you don't. That's impossible!'),
> that they meant X by what they said ('Nah, you only say you do, but there's really no such thing as meaning anything by one's words!'),
> that they knew what a given word meant ('You say you know what *bicycle* means, but you really don't!'),
> that, in speaking they are expressing their thoughts ('Of course you aren't; that would be impossible!').
> And so on.

Anyone who made a regular habit of this, would probably receive the sarcastic reply: 'Get a life!' Pretty quickly, they'd lose what friends they had; and if they kept it up, they would probably be put under psychiatric supervision in a mental hospital. Now, imagine if *we all* did this, and we did it *all of the time*. Everyday interaction—and so life as we know it—would collapse.

The sentences listed under 1-8 above—from which emerges the commonsense picture of communication—are derived from the repeated, uncontroversial utterance of metadiscursive remarks like 9-16. As an example, take sentence 1 again. It is a perfectly ordinary and uncontroversial occurrence for people to say, in particular circumstances, that they understand someone else, as in 9. This doesn't mean that no one ever objects to particular instances of such claims. Of course they do. However, communicational interaction would be nothing like we know it to be if we all always objected whenever someone was said to understand what someone else said. Consequently, it seems perfectly justifiable to us to make the general claim given in 1: 'We usually understand what we say to each other.'

In other words, the assignment of the status of commonsense truism to sentence 1—and, hence, the theorist's assumption of the existence of the *reality* he takes it to describe—is motivated by the fact that it would be absurd to deny (i.e. to declare false) the countless instances of metadiscursive commonplaces like 9. Moreover, if called upon to justify the truth of the general statement 1, this would most naturally be done by reference to the accepted truth of the particular metadiscursive remarks. (Would it not be nonsense to agree that commonplaces like 9 are usually true yet to deny the truth of 1?) If it would be absurd *regularly* to deny particular instances of 'We understand each other', then it would be no less absurd to deny the general statement 'We usually understand what we say to each other.' And the same goes for the metadiscursive remarks 10 through 16, and their corresponding components of the commonsense picture.

So, 'ordinary life' would appear to exclude as a viable attitude (outside of the philosophy classroom) the sceptical treat-ment of claims such as 1-8. Consequently, it should come as no surprise that those who reflect 'seriously' on the topic of language and communication typically begin by taking for granted (a) the truth of those claims and (b) the existence of the communicational reality that, if the claims *are* true, they are true *of*. The point of a theory of language, then, is to describe and explain that taken-for-granted communicational reality. Hence the rhetorical strangle-hold that the commonsense picture of language has on the discursive construction of theories of language. In other words, according to the rhetorical perspective adopted in this paper, it is here that we may locate an answer to the question why we (in the Western intellectual tradition) need a theory of language.

Now, if—as I have argued—the language theorist cannot, without courting absurdity, *deny* the commonsense picture of language and communication and if the legacy of *affirming* that picture can only be the repeated regeneration of the same frustrating rhetorical puzzles and similarly unproductive 'solutions' to those puzzles, is there, therefore, no hope of redirecting theoretical reflection on language towards more positive ends? Is my conclusion that the rhetorical force of the commonsense picture is such that theoretical reflection on language must *necessarily* remain a fruitless form of intellectual discourse?

No, this is not the message with which I would like to leave the readers of this paper. I hope that the picture I have presented of the ever-regenerative rhetorical source of language theory will instead motivate the following conclusion. If language theory is to avoid the rhetorical legacy of the commonsense picture, we must focus our energies on addressing the rhetorical source of that picture. And this, as I have just argued, lies in the interpretation of everyday metadiscursive remarks—such as 9-16—as generalizable, empirical propositions. In other words, as long as it is taken for granted that, when we say such things as

'We understand each other',

> '*Soporific* means "attending to produce sleep"', and
> 'You know English as well as I do',

the communicational relevance of these utterances is appropriately characterized by reference to particular states of affairs the obtaining of which *justifies* their assertion—that is

> our state of mutual understanding,
> the meaning of *soporific*, and
> our mutual knowledge of the English language—

then the first step will already have been taken down a well-trodden rhetorical path leading inexorably, via the conceptual picture we call 'commonsense', to the familiar problems and paradigms of the Western linguistic tradition. If we are to avoid taking this first step—and so avoid its rhetorical consequences—we must try to develop alternative ways of understanding, and expressing our understanding, of the relevance of practical metadiscourse to the interactional construction of everyday talk. An essential prerequisite to any fruitful dialogue between linguists and philosophers of language is the identification of those problems generated in both disciplines by failure to examine in depth the role of our lay metadiscursive practices. Until this need is recognized, linguistics and philosophy will continue to have little to offer each other apart from alternative ways of getting lost in the same rhetorical labyrinth.

References

Condillac, E. B. (1947) *Œuvres philosophiques*, vol. 1. Edited by G. le Roy. Paris: Presses Universitaires de France.

Condillac, E. B. (1981) *La langue des calculs*. Edited by S. Auroux and A.-M. Chouillet. Lille: Presses Universitaires de Lille.

Frege, G. (1979) *Posthumous Writings*. Oxford: Blackwell.
Frege, G. (1984) *Collected Writings on Mathematics, Logic and Philosophy*. Oxford: Blackwell.
Heritage, J. (1984) *Garfinkel and Ethnomethodology*. Cambridge: Polity Press.
Locke, J. (1690) *Essay Concerning Human Understanding*. Edited by P. H. Nidditch. Oxford: Clarendon Press, 1975.
Saussure, F. de (1916) *Cours de linguistique générale* (2nd éd., 1922). English translation by R. Harris. London: Duckworth, 1983.
Saussure, F. de (1974) *Cours de linguistique générale*, vol. 2. Critical edition by R. Engler. Wiesbaden: Otto Harrassowitz.
Sperber, D. and Wilson, D. (1986) *Relevance: Communication and Cognition*. Oxford: Blackwell.
Taylor, T. J. (1992) *Mutual Misunderstanding: Scepticism and the Theorizing of Language and Interpretation*. Durham, N. C : Duke University Press and London: Routledge.

V

Folk Psychology and the Language Myth: What would the integrationist say?

Am I conscious? Do you believe that you are reading this sentence? Do you intend to read the whole article? When I say 'Austin Powers', do you know to whom I am referring? Did you understand what I just said?

An intriguing characteristic of 20th century psychology and the philosophy of mind is the debate whether such questions make any sense. For many psychologists and philosophers claim that such commonsense questions are nonsensical, have no determinate meaning, or have only the meanings of myths and primitive superstitions. Such questions, they say, are the product of a folk psychology that has long dominated Western thinking about the mind, the components of which, if the sciences of the mind are ever to progress, need to be eliminated not only from scientific theories of the mind but also from everyday talk. These Eliminativists—including the behaviourist pschologist J.B. Watson and the philosophers Paul Churchland and Stephen Stich—argue that the notions that populate folk psychological discourse—notions such as 'belief', 'wish', 'know', 'desire', 'refer', 'understand'—are "the heritages of a timid savage past", handed down, generation after generation, at mother's knee (Watson 1924: 3). These notions and the folk reasoning which makes use of them ought to be assigned the same fate as was meted out, following the birth of modern chemistry, to alchemical notions such as 'phlogiston', 'caloric', and 'essences'. As some leading Eliminativists explain:

> Eliminativism .... is the claim that some category of entities, processes, or properties exploited in a commonsense or scientific account of the world do not exist. (Ramsey, Stich, and Garon 1991: 94)

> Folk psychology they say is the theory of mind that has dominated Western culture for many centuries. Moreover, as John Searle points out, there are signs of its influence in non-Western culture as well – as the Dalai Lama apparently holds such a theory (Searle 1999: 52)

This paper concerns the opposition between Eliminativists and (what I shall call) Anti-Eliminativists in modern philosophy of mind: i.e., those who claim that terms such as 'belief', 'intend', 'refer', 'mean' and remarks such as "He believes I'm crazy" should not be banished either from modern cognitive psychology or from lay psychological discourse. But in addition to this explanatory goal, the paper is intended to raise two questions. First, what is the connection between the Language Myth (Harris 1981) and the arguments for and against eliminativism in contemporary philosophy of mind? Second, because it is easy to see the overlap between the concepts of so-called 'folk psychology' and those of what we might call 'folk linguistics', we can ask the following question: What should be the integrational linguist's position on folk psychology and folk linguistics? Specifically, should all, some, or none of the constitutive concepts be retained in the integrational study of language and communication? Should one of the integrationist's goals be to show what meaning, understanding, reference, belief, etc., really are – that is, properly seen within an integrationist approach that has freed itself from the influence of the Language Myth? Or, should the goal be to replace these conceptual and terminological legacies of the Language Myth (and perhaps other Western cultural myths) with terms and concepts that (a) are motivated directly by the integrational approach and (b) do not 'carry with them' the conceptual baggage of the Language Myth?

To put it bluntly: Should the integrationist aim to explain what it is to mean, to understand, to believe, to refer, to be a sign, etc? Or should this not be one of the integrationist's aims, on the grounds that those terms are too infected by the Language Myth?

Early Eliminativists
What have the Eliminativists got against folk psychology? Some of the earliest Eliminativists were members of the behaviourist school and saw the rejection of 'commonsense' psychological terms and reasoning as a necessary stage in their efforts to make psychology into a proper science. J.B. Watson argued that to become truly scientific, psychology had to purge from its conceptual foundations all 'commonsense' psychological notions and folklore about why people do what they do. These concepts and familiar platitudes of psychological explanation are the cultural legacy of folk traditions, religion, and mythological notions about the mind and its putative contents. Just as progress in other sciences required the purging

of commonsense assumptions, concepts, and explanations, the same, Watson argued, is required for psychology to become a true science. And yet, he complained, the introspectionist theories that had hitherto dominated psychological research had done the reverse: they had taken for granted the legitimacy of commonsense psychology. Introspectionist psychology presupposes the existence of genuine psychological phenomena which are the purported referents for such common-sense terms as 'belief', 'consciousness', 'desire', etc. And it assumes that a subject's reports of what he experiences, believes, or desires—or of why he behaved as he did—represent, ceteris paribus, actual mental states – the very mental states that the introspectionist takes to be the objects of psychological investigation.

For instance, in his book *Behaviorism* (Watson 1924: 4), Watson criticizes William James' reliance on 'commonsense' in the definition of the science of psychology. The definition that James gives is "Psychology is the description and explanation of states of consciousness as such." But Watson objects that this definition begs the question of the existence of states of consciousness — the question, that is, whether there really are any mental phenomena referred to by the term 'states of consciousness'. Furthermore, Watson accuses James of diverting the reader's attention from this weakness in his definition by rhetorical sleight of hand: namely, by invoking the commonsense, 'everybody-knows' character of the concept of consciousness (Watson 1924: 4). In James' own words

> [When we] look into our own minds and report what we there discover....[e]veryone agrees that we there discover states of consciousness. So far as I know, the existence of such states has never been doubted by any critic, however sceptical in other respects he may have been..... All people unhesitatingly believe that they feel

themselves thinking and that they distinguish the mental state. (...) I regard this belief as the most fundamental of all the postulates of Psychology. (James 1890: 185)

"Consciousness – Oh, yes, everybody must know what this 'consciousness' is" is Watson's sarcastic reply (Watson 1924: 4). And yet, Watson argued:

[C]onsciousness is neither a definite nor a usable concept. (...) [B]elief in the existence of consciousness goes back to the ancient days of superstition and myth. (...) The great mass of people even today want to believe in magic. (...) As time goes on, all of these critically undigested, innumerable told tales get woven into the folk lore of the people." (Watson 1924: 2)

Watson saw folk psychology as a form of mythification, religious superstition, and magic. Its familiar patterns of reasoning and explanation he characterized as consisting in nothing but the "old wives' tales" that each new generation learns and then passes down to the next generation "as gospel" (Watson 1924: 2). Scientific psychology could never be constructed on such mythical foundations. Its whole ontology, epistemology, and logic had to be rejected in order that a true science of human behaviour could at last be constructed on firm foundations.

Contemporary Eliminativists argue that folk psychology is a theory

Today, proponents of eliminativism take a different tack from Watson while still arguing for the same eliminativist conclusion. In the first place, the central figures in the folk psychology debate today are physicalists. That is, whereas Watson took behaviour to be the explanatory object for the science of psychology, they take physical properties and processes in the brain as the ultimate explanatory objects for scientific psychology. Secondly, whereas Watson described commonsense talk about the mind and its contents as a kind of folklore and mythology, today's Eliminativists argue that commonsense remarks about the mind are theoretical claims or hypotheses. That is, the layperson's remarks about what they believe, what they know, what they refer to or understand, etc, are the 'products' of an underlying theory. 'Folk psychology' is the name given to this theory. A leading Eliminativist, Stephen Stich says:

> In our everyday dealings with one another we invoke a variety of commonsense psychological terms including 'belief', 'remember', 'feel', 'think', 'desire', 'prefer', 'imagine', 'fear', and many others. The use of these terms is governed by a loose network of largely tacit principles, platitudes, and paradigms which constitute a sort of folk theory. (Stich 1983: 1)

Stich's point, in other words, is that when the long-suffering Bloggs says that Daniel believes that Neptune is at a mathematically predicatable distance from Uranus, Bloggs is uttering a hypothesis. The sense of this hypothesis is a function of the underlying psychological theory, a theory which determines the conceptual content denoted by its component terms (e.g. the term of 'belief'), the logical syntax of the propositions formed with those terms, and the implicational relations between those propositions. Bloggs' utterance thus attributes to Daniel what is sometimes called a 'propositional attitude' or 'intentional state' — namely 'believing that Neptune is at a mathematically predicatable distance from Uranus'. As a hypothesis it is true if that propositional attitude is somehow represented in Daniel's brain, false if it is not. Eliminativists such as Stich point out that to take such an utterance to be true is to presuppose an ontology of particular brain states or events – namely, those that must obtain for the sentence to be true.

In other words, Eliminativists (although not only Elimi-nativists) maintain that in taking ordinary psychological remarks to be true, we make an ontological commitment to the existence of particular neurological states or events – the very ones that must obtain for those remarks to be true.

Eliminativists argue that folk psychology needs replacement

The Eliminativist's central thesis is that not only is folk psychological discourse the 'output' of an underlying theory of the mind, that theory is a bad theory. As another leading Eliminativist puts it:

> Folk Psychology is false and its ontology is chimerical. Beliefs and desires are of a piece with phlogiston, caloric, and the alchemical essences. (Churchland 1991: 65)

There are, in other words, no such things as beliefs, meanings, thoughts, fears, desires, and intentions. There is no such neurological state as 'believing TJT is crazy' or 'understanding what I just said'. This at any rate is what the contemporary cognitive neurosciences are discovering: i.e., that no brain states or events are identifiable as corresponding to the folk terms 'intention', 'meaning', 'thought' or to propositional attitudes such as 'believing that Neptune is at a mathematically predicatable distance from Uranus'. Furthermore, given what is being discovered about the physical properties of the brain, it is seen as increasingly unlikely that such states or events ever will be identifiable. To put it bluntly: they just aren't there, so we should give up looking for them. From this, the modern Eliminativist concludes that, just as the terms 'phlogiston', 'caloric', and 'alchemical essence' were abandoned as modern chemistry discovered that they had no referents, so folk psychological terms should be dropped – for, like all mythical terms, they refer to nothing at all. The same goes for statements such as "Henry VIII believed that Pope Clement would allow the annulment of his marriage to Catherine of Aragon". Stephen Stich put the matter thus:

> Did Henry VIII believe that Pope Clement would allow the annulment of his marriage to Catherine of Aragon? ...... [T]he question has no answer. Beliefs are myths, and it is no more sensible to inquire about Henry's beliefs than to investigate whether he had an excess of phlegm or a deficiency of yellow bile. (Stich 1983: 2)

As a bad theory, with a chimerical ontology, the Eliminativist Paul Churchland argues that folk psychology should be—and eventually will be—replaced by the much improved psychological theories being developed in contemporary cognitive science.
"Folk psychology is a radically inadequate account of our internal activities, too confused and too defective..... It will simply be displaced by a better theory of those activities." (Churchland 1981: 72)

'Commonsense' resistance to Eliminativism
The Anti-eliminativist position draws on the rhetorical power of 'commonsense' in resisting Eliminativist arguments. Folk psychology has to be protected from sceptical attack. Of course we believe, fear and desire, are conscious, have intentions, mean things by our words, and understand each other.

Of course Daniel believes that Neptune is at a mathematically predicatable distance from Uranus.

To get a taste of the rhetorical power of such 'commonsense' defenses of folk psychology, consider the alternative of denying an instance of a folk psychological claim. Suppose we say that Henry VIII believed that the Pope would resist his efforts to divorce Catherine of Aragon. But the Eliminativist says that there are no such intentional states as 'believing such-and-such'. OK, well, if beliefs are no more than myths, then ought we to say that Henry did not believe the Pope would resist his efforts to divorce Catherine? Or that he had no such belief? Would it not be absurd to insist that reading this article is not something you are doing intentionally – since there are no such things as intentions? Or that you do not understand any of the words I am using – since there is no such thing as understanding? Or that you are not in fact conscious? After all, if consciousness really is a myth, then how can it be true that you are conscious? But 'commonsense' supposedly tells us that such sceptical claims are absurd, doesn't it? Doubtless anyone who went around asserting that no one believes anything, that no one is conscious, that no one understands anything, that no one means anything would—if her daily behaviour scrupulously accorded with these claims—end up being sent to a psychiatrist and might well never be seen outside the mental asylum again.

However, it is worth emphasizing that the Anti-Elimina-tivists agree with the Eliminativists that if it is justifiable to assert that Henry believed that the Pope would resist, this is simply because *it is true*: Henry really did believe that. Furthermore, they both agree that the matter whether Henry really did or really didn't believe that is independent of anyone's *assertion* of what Henry believed. In other words, there must be *grounds* for this assertion—some conditions the obtaining of which justify the assertion (*if* it is justified)—and these grounds must be independent of the assertion itself. But it is here where the Anti-eliminativist school splits into different camps: i.e., on the issue of what conditions must obtain for an assertion such as "He believes the Pope will resist" to be true. In the following I will identify these two camps of Anti-Eliminativists as the Realists and the Anti-Realists.

Intentional Realism

John Searle strongly resists the sceptical stance of the Eliminati-vists. He starts from the position that folk psychological discourse *must*, in general, be true "or we would not have survived" (Searle 1992: 59). Moreover, he accepts that the truth of a folk attribution of a particular mental ('intentional') state, say Henry's belief, depends on the existence in Henry's head of a particular physical state, namely that brain state in which his belief consists. Searle's preferred example concerns not the lusty English monarch of Herman's Hermits fame but a more modern head of state who nevertheless suffers from a similar sort of problem. Searle says:

> Suppose I now believe, as I do, that Clinton is president of the United States. Whatever else that belief might be, it is a state of my brain .... consisting in such things as configurations of neurons and synaptic connections, activated by neurotransmitters. (Searle 1999: 89-90)

Searle accepts that neuroscientists have not yet identified the particular brain states in which beliefs or any other intentional states consist. He even appears to accept that neuroscience may never successfully reduce intentional states to brain states. But this question, he insists, "is irrelevant to the question of their existence" (Searle 1992: 60). Intentional states, he maintains, have subjective, phenomenological characteristics which may not be identifiable with the tools and techniques currently available in neuroscience.

Another intentional realist, Jerry Fodor, rejects the 'phenomenological' implications of Searle's position, but still resists eliminativist scepticism about propositional attitudes.

> [T]he present interpretation of the relation between neurological and psychological constructs is compatible with very strong claims about the ineliminability of mental language from behavioural theories. (Fodor 1968: 116)

However, Fodor argues that a given belief consists not in a particular brain state but rather in an indefinite set of possibly heterogeneous brain states that are, nonetheless, 'functionally equivalent'. What makes these brain states functionally equivalent is that they enter into the same causal relations – causal relations whose behavioural outcomes are characterized in the same folk psychological terms.

> [I]dentical psychological functions [can] sometimes be ascribed to anatomically heterogeneous neural mechanisms. In that case mental language will be required to state the conditions upon such ascriptions of functional equivalence. (...)
>
> Every mousetrap can be identified with some mechanism, and being a mousetrap can therefore be identifed with being a member of some (indefinite) set of possible mechanisms. But enumerating the set is not a way of dispensing with the notion of a mousetrap; that notion is required to say what all the members of the set have in common and, in particular, what credentials would be required to certify a putative new member as belonging to the set. (Fodor 1968: 116-17)

In other words, if we eliminate folk psychological discourse from neuropsychological investigations, we will have no way of classifying any states of the brain as the same or different, at least not in a way with any relevance to explaining human behaviour. Brain states, according to Fodor, simply are categorized by their functional characteristics; and without folk psychological terms to use in characterizing their behavioural outcomes, those categories will not be identifiable.

Searle and Fodor can be seen as protecting folk psychology from the sceptical attacks of the Eliminativists, but it should be clear that this 'protection' is bought at a metaphysical cost. In the first place, they both beg the question of the truth of folk psychological claims. Searle uses a counterfactual conditional in asserting that folk psychological claims 'have to be' true: that is, they have to be true because otherwise we human beings would not have survived. Such a rhetorical maneuver puts the onus on the sceptic to show that, in fact, we *could* have survived even if no folk psychological claim were true. But how is the poor sceptic to do this? Fodor, on the other hand, takes the truth of folk psychological claims for granted and, to provide something that they can be true of, he conjures up the notion of 'functionally equivalent' brain states, which is what intentional claims are really 'about'. Moreover, the functional equivalence of these brain states will only be identifiable if folk psychological terms *remain* a central tool of neuropsychological investigation. With this argument, Fodor can be seen to push the realist envelope as far as it can conceivably go. To go any further than this is to enter the domain of Anti-Realism, where Daniel Dennett may be found happily residing.

Anti-Realism/Instrumentalism
Dennett has many times made clear his agreement with the Eliminativists' scepticism about the existence of *referents* for folk psychological expressions.

> I believe [it] to be false ... that our ordinary way of picking out putative mental features and entities succeeds in picking out real features and entities. (...) About ... putative mental entities [such as beliefs and desires] I am an eliminative materialist." (Dennett 1981: xix-xx)

However, it is important to note that Dennett is not suggesting that folk psychological *discourse* ought to be revised or replaced, nor that familiar terms like 'belief' and 'intention' ought to be eliminated. Rather, it is the theorization of such folk psychological terms that is the real culprit. As the following passage illustrates, Dennett thinks that folk psychological terms can lead— and repeatedly have led—theorists to postulate a "confused ontology" of mental states in the head. It is these putative mental entities, thus theorized into ideological existence, whose elimination he argues for.

> Suppose we find a society that lacks our knowledge of human physiology, and that speaks a language just like English except for one curious family of idioms. When they are tired they talk of being beset by *fatigues*, of having mental fatigues, muscular fatigues, fatigues in the eyes and fatigues of the spirit. Their sports lore contains such maxims as "too many fatigues spoils your aim" and "five fatigues in the legs are worth ten in the arms". When we encounter them and tell them of our science, they want to know *what fatigues are*. They have been puzzling over such questions as whether numerically the same fatigue can come and go and return, whether fatigues have a definite location in matter and space and time, whether fatigues are identical with some particular physical states or processes or events in their bodies, or are made of some sort of stuff.

> We can see that they are off to a bad start with these questions, but what should we tell them? One thing we might tell them is that there simply are no such things as fatigues – they have a confused ontology. We can expect some of them to retort: "You don't think there are fatigues? Run around the block a few times and you'll know better! There are many things your science might teach us, but the non-existence of fatigues isn't one of them!"
>
> We ought to be unmoved by this retort, but if we wanted to acknowledge this society's "right" to go on talking about fatigues—it's their language, after all—we might try to accommodate by agreeing to call at least some of the claims they make about fatigues true and false, depending on whether the relevant individuals are drowsy, exhausted or feigning, etc. We could then give as best we could the physiological conditions for the truth and falsity of those claims, but refuse to take the apparent ontology of those claims seriously. (...) Fatigues are not good theoretical entities, however well entrenched the term 'fatigues' is in the habits of thought of the imagined society. The same is true, I hold, of beliefs, desires, pains, mental images, experiences – as all these are *ordinarily* understood. Not only are *beliefs* and *pains* not good theoretical *things* (like electrons or neurons), but the *state-of-believing-that-p* is not a well-defined or definable theoretical *state*. (Dennett 1981: xix-xx)

Given this sceptical conclusion, one might initially be surprised to hear that, all the same, Dennett characterizes the 'intentional stance'—the notion whose virtues he trumpets in all his writings—as "the view from folk psychology" (Dennett 1996: 27; Dennett 1981: 3). Moreover, it is the intentional stance which, according to Dennett, allows us to recognize our fellow humans (and some other animals) as 'intentional systems', a recognition on which all of our moral thought, cultural behaviour, and self-understanding depend. In other words, it is essential to our understanding of our own and others' behaviour and of the social worlds within which we live and act that we conceive of ourselves as creatures who believe, who desire, who think, who intend, who mean, and who understand. In other words, we cannot give up thinking of ourselves as 'intentional systems'. That is, we cannot give up the view from folk psychology.

> An intentional system is a system whose behaviour can be explained and predicted by relying on ascriptions to the system of beliefs and desires and other intentionally characterized features... hopes, fears, intentions, perceptions, expectations, etc." (Dennett 1981: 271)

Dennett therefore is an ardent defender of folk psychology. In the following extract from one of his published defenses, he illustrates the importance of the intentional stance to our understanding of ordinary human abilities, such as the ability to understand a joke.

> *'A man went to visit his friend the Newfie and found him with both ears bandaged. "What happened?" he asked, and the Newfie replied, "I was ironing my shirt, you know, and the telephone rang." "That explains one ear, but what about the other?" "Well, you know, I had to call the doctor!'*
> If we.... ask what one has to believe in order to get the joke,...what we get is a long list of different propositions. You must have beliefs about the shape of an iron, the shape of a telephone; the fact that when

people are stupid, they often cannot coordinate the left hand with the right hand doing different things; the fact that the hefts of a telephone receiver and an iron are approximately the same; the fact that when telephones ring, people generally answer them; and many more.

What makes my narrative a joke and not just a boring story is that ...it leaves out many facts and counts on your filling them in, but you could fill them in only if you had all those beliefs. (...) Strike off one belief on that list and see what happens. That is, find some people who do not have the belief (but have all the others), and tell them the joke. They will not get it. They cannot get it, because each of the beliefs is necessary for comprehension of the story. (Dennett 1991: 139-40)

This argument may seem to sit oddly with the Eliminativism that Dennett often advocates. For on those occasions, he is arguing sceptically that an intentional term like 'belief' has no referent. Like the use of the term 'fatigues' in the first passage I quoted, the use of 'beliefs' suggests a 'confused ontology'. Yet in his analysis of what is required to understand the Newfie joke he appears to be arguing that one *must* have beliefs in order to get the joke, and of course the unspoken assumption is that we *do* get the joke. So, how can it be that we have beliefs and yet that the term 'belief' has no referent?

The answer to this conundrum lies in Dennett's Anti-Realism. For his point is not that there must be such *thing*s (mental entities) as beliefs but that it must be legitimate to *claim* that people—e.g., those of his readers who get this joke—have beliefs. Ascriptions of belief, of intentions, of desires, of meanings, and of understanding are essential to our ability to understand ourselves and our behaviour. Belief-claims, for instance, cannot be eliminated from discourse without thereby losing our ability to make sense of what it is to get a joke and what doing so requires. Belief-claims are necessary, but they should not be interpreted on a theoretical model. It is better, Dennett argues, to conceive of folk psychological discourse *not* as the manifestation of a folk theory but rather as a form of "folk craft" (Dennett 1991: 135). It is a craft—a discursive technique—for predicting and explaining human behaviour. It is the mediating instrument of the intentional stance. And this leads Dennett to affirm its use not only with regard to human behaviour. For he claims to see no objection to using the same folk psychological terms in characterizing the behaviour of computers. Moreover, it is the legitimacy of characterizing computers in such terms that leads to the conclusion that a computer, like a human and some other animals, is an intentional system.

> The computer is an intentional system ... not because it has any particular intrinsic features, and not because it really and truly has beliefs and desires (whatever that would be), but just because it succumbs to a certain *stance* adopted toward it, namely the intentional stance, the stance that proceeds by ascribing intentional predicates under the usual constraints to the computer.... (Dennett 1981: 273)

Folk Psychology and the Language Myth
How are these debates about 'folk psychology' related to the Language Myth? The Language Myth is the assumption that discourse—in this case folk psychological discourse—is understandable because those participating in the discourse know and use a fixed code. This code determines the meanings of the words and sentences used in the discourse. Well, if this is how discourse using words like 'belief', 'intention', 'consciousness', and 'understanding' is understandable, then the

question naturally arises: What precisely are the meanings that the code assigns to these words? And what are the meanings of sentences such as "He believes I'm crazy", "He intends to resign", and "I understand what you said"?

Surrogationalism (Harris 1980) is a characteristically Western-cultural corollary to the Language Myth. It is the assumption that the meaning of a word is what it 'stands for' and that the meaning of a sentence is the set of circumstances or state of affairs which the sentence is 'about' – or, according to a common formulation, those circumstances which must obtain in order for the sentence to be true. In the debates about folk psychology, it seems clear that Realists such as Searle and Fodor take for granted

> (i) the legitimacy of folk psychological discourse
>   ("Otherwise how could we have survived?") and
> (ii) the surrogationalist explanation of that legitimacy.

In other words, they assume that many of the assertions of folk psychological discourse are true and that this is because the circumstances which their truth requires do in fact obtain. Given this assumption, the Realists naturally conclude that

> (a) there *must* be something that mental terms such as 'belief' and 'understand' stand for and
> (b) there must be brain states which folk psychological assertions are about and which, in the case of true assertions, do in fact obtain.

Of course, as we have seen, Searle and Fodor differ over the phenomenological or functional identity of these brain states, but the conclusion that they *must* be real is shared by both. Not surprisingly, they conclude that it is these neurological realities that should be the objects of scientific psychology.

The Eliminativist, on the other hand, shares the Realist's surrogationalist premise, although he sceptically refuses to take for granted the legitimacy of folk psychological discourse. So he turns to the empirical findings of scientific research to determine if the brain states required to legitimate folk psychological assertions do in fact obtain. However, neuropsychological research has not succeeded in identifying any plausible neurological candidates *either* for referents of folk psychological terms *or* for truth-conditions for folk psychological assertions. In other words, neuropsychological research has not found anything which the components of folk psychological discourse could plausibly be construed to be 'about'. Therefore, the Eliminativist argues that, *not really being about anything at all*, folk psychological discourse ought to be radically revised – including the elimination of many of its most familiar terms and locutions. If this is not done, argues the Eliminativist, then we will continue to be fooled into retaining the mythological assumption that folk psychological discourse is in fact about something real—that there really are such things as thoughts and intentions—and that people really do believe, mean, understand, and imagine. Worst of all, the onus will remain on the long-suffering neuroscientists to find and explain the properties of these entirely mythical entities and states.

Another characteristically Western corollary to the Language Myth (Harris 1980) is what Harris calls 'instrumentalism'. Instrumentalism offers an alternative to the surrogationalist account of how language means. According to the instrumentalist, meaning inheres in a word or sentence's usefulness for interactional purposes. The Anti-Realist in the debate, such as Dan Dennett, shares the Realist's assumption of the legitimacy of folk psychological discourse; but he rejects the Realist's assumption that that legitimacy inheres in the surrogational properties of that discourse. On the contrary, he advocates the instrumentalist view that folk psychological discourse is legitimate simply *because it is interactionally useful*. This is Dennett's argument in claiming that folk psychology is a "calculus" for predicting and explaining the behaviour of others. "X believes that snow is white if X can be predicatively attributed the belief that snow is white." (Dennett 1981: xvii). Folk psychological terms and assertions do not mean by representing or 'standing for' neurological entities or states of affairs, but rather as a function of their usefulness in mediating and managing our daily interactional lives with others. The evolutionary advantage of this instrumentalist 'calculus' is assumed by Dennett to be obvious, just as Searle assumes it to be obvious that without folk psychology, humanity would not have survived.

The Anti-Realist therefore concludes that it is mistaken to conclude that folk psychological terms should be eliminated simply because neuroscientists can find no referents for them in the brain. Moreover, it is a surrogationalist mistake. From the Anti-Realist's instrumentalist perspective, it is hardly surprising that neuroscientists cannot find anything for folk psychological terms to stand for. But, so what? As the Anti-Realist sees it, folk psychological discourse can still mean as satisfactorily as other forms of discourse do, as a function of its usefulness in the attainment of human communicational goals.

* * *

As integrational linguistics matures in its role as the not-so-loyal opposition to mainstream linguistics, it may find that there is much to be learned from the rhetorical knots into which cognitive psychologists and philosophers have tied themselves over the issue of folk psychology. For it would seem that the same kinds of questions that psychologists and philosophers take to be raised by folk psychological discourse could also be seen to be posed by so-called 'folk' linguistic discourse. How should the integrationist respond to these questions? (For an extended discussion of how mainstream, or 'orthodox', linguistics has responded to them, see Taylor 1992.) Should the integrationist also adopt an Eliminativist stance toward such everyday meta-discursive terms as 'meaning', 'understands', 'refers', 'the English language', etc.? That is, should she argue that there are no such things as meanings or languages, that understanding and referring are not real-world, mental, or any other kind of event, and that it would therefore be better to throw these terms—and language-games concerning them—on the same rubbish heap where have long lain the terms 'phlogiston' and 'caloric'? Or should the integrationist adopt a revitalized form of Realism, perhaps arguing that of course there are such things as meanings and languages and that people really do understand each other and mean what they say, albeit not always? The problem, the Realist integrationist could then claim, is not with the terms themselves nor with the ordinary, 'folk' use of them nor with the things or events they refer to, but rather with the family of orthodox linguistic theories that have conspicuously failed to say anything sensible about them in the over two thousand years of the Western linguistic tradition. The Realist integrationist's task, therefore, would be to say what meaning, understanding, languages, etc., *really are*—when clearly seen from outside the mystifying confines of orthodox linguistic theorizing. Or, lastly, should the integrationist opt for an Anti-Realist position, arguing perhaps, like Dennett, that while reality (of whatever ontological flavour) *does not in fact* contain such things as meanings and languages, nor events such as understanding and referring, nevertheless, these are essential components of 'our' (Western-cultural) way of conceptualizing and enacting human language? And that therefore, they should not be eliminated, but just re-thought and re-defined?

Doubtless it would be better to put these questions in more general terms, extracting them from the web of *a priori* assumptions and conceptions that have influenced the strategies adopted in the folk psychology debate – those assumptions and conceptions that have contributed to the absurd character of some of the popular academic positions discussed above. So, to put the matter more generally, we might ask: Should the integrationist's goal be to determine, for instance, what *signs* really are, in contrast to the faulty descriptions given by theorists influenced by the Language Myth? Should the integrationist take it as a goal to give a Language-Myth-free explanation of what it is for an utterance to *mean* something? Or what it is for a speaker to *refer* to something or someone or to *mean* what he says? Or what it is for one person to *understand* what another says? Or what it is to be *a language*? Or what it is for a language to *change*? Or, on the other hand, should the integrationist advocate the elimination of these language-myth-and-Western-culture-infected terms and concepts from integrational theories of language and communication? My hope is that these questions will enliven the discourse of integrationism in the coming years.

References

Churchland, P. (1981) "Eliminative materialism and the propositional attitudes". *Journal of Philosophy*, vol.78, no.2

Churchland, P. (1991) "Folk psychology and the explanation of human behaviour" In Greenwood 1991.

Dennett, D. (1981) *Brainstorms,* Cambridge, Mass.: MIT Press.

Dennett, D. (1991) "Two contrasts: folk craft versus folk science, and belief versus opinion " In Greenwood 1991.

Dennett, D. (1996) *Kinds of Minds*, New York: Basic Books.
Fodor, J. (1968) *Psychological Explanation,* New York: Ran-dom House.
Greenwood, J.D. (Ed.) (1991) *The Future of Folk Psychology*, Cambridge: Cambridge University Press.
Harris, R. (1980) *The Language Makers*, London: Duckworth.
Harris, R. (1981) *The Language Myth,* London: Duckworth.
James, W. (1890) *Principles of Psychology,* London: Henry Holt & Co.
Ramsey, W., S. Stich, and J. Garon (1991) "Connectionism, eliminativism, and the future of folk psychology". In Greenwood 1991.
Searle, J. (1992) *The Rediscovery of Mind,* Cambridge, Mass.: MIT Press.
Searle, J. (1999) *Mind, Language, and Society,* London: Weidenfield & Nicolson.
Stich, S. (1983) *From Folk Psychology to Cognitive Science*, Cambridge, Mass.: MIT Press.
Taylor, T.J. (1992) *Mutual Misunderstanding: Scepticism and the Theorizing of Language and Interpretation*, Durham, N.C.: Duke University Press and London: Routledge.
Watson, J. (1924) *Behaviourism*, Chicago: University of Chicago Press.

VI

Talking about what happened

In the context of a volume on language and history certain questions seem to me worthy of our consideration. An obvious question is that which forms the topic of historical linguistics. Another is the question of the origin and evolution of human language. I am not going to touch on these questions here. Instead, I will begin with the avowedly simplistic premise that history is a matter of *what happened*. Of course, historians do not merely report or describe what happened. They also

- explain why it happened,
- analyze the conditions that led to its happening,
- trace the relationships between what happened at one time and what happened at another,
- propose principles or forces which are said to direct the course of historical events,
- and more...

Still, keeping to the most general level, it seems fair to say that history is a matter of "what happened". And, of course, this applies to both the ontological and the epistemological senses of the term "history". In other words, in addressing questions of history, we are addressing questions about historical events *themselves* and also questions about what historians and others *assert* about historical events.

At this point I ought to say something about the sorts of questions about language-and-history that particularly attract my own attention. However, I admit straightaway that the points touched on in this chapter are already very well-known, both to linguists and historians. My intention here is simply to foreground certain themes in preparation for the main part of my discussion.

First, it would seem appropriate to begin with a question that concerns the place of language *in* historical happenings. If we take history in its most general and commonsense terms to be a matter of what happened, we can ask "How was language part of what happened?" After all, historical events very often involve language.

- *Churchill was told in advance that the Germans were going to bomb Coventry.*
- *The American naval captain John Paul Jones shouted across the water to the British captain that he would never give up his ship.*
- *General Douglas MacArthur declared to the Philippine people "I shall return."*
- *President John F. Kennedy informed the Berlin people that he was a jelly doughnut.*

Naturally, then, the historical events and circumstances addressed by historians often involve language. And this raises a question: Given that the work of historians begins with descriptions and statements of what happened, how should they address the roles that language plays in those historical events?

Of course, there are also historical events—with or without the participation of humans—which do not involve language. It seems obvious that these two—events *with* and events *without* language—should not be treated identically, that is, that the former pose an extra layer of issues and questions not raised by the latter. If we take this difference as a given, then what should the historian do to account for it? When language is present, how should the historian approach the role that it played in 'what happened'?

A second question, related to this first, is one that can be, and, indeed, increasingly is, raised about language and history. This question concerns *talking about* historical events, whether this talk (or writing) occurs at the same general time of the events themselves or at a later time. This question can be put as follows: What effect does the way that we characterize an historical event have in how we treat that event? I have cautiously put that final clause— "how we treat that event"— in very vague terms. But some theorists today are less cautious and would put this question in a more specific form: How and to what extent is what-we-say-about an historical event constitutive of the event? Or: how does what-we-say-about-it construct the event?

Personally, I am sceptical about the manner of speaking in which language or a particular use of language is said somehow to be "constitutive" of an historical event, or to "construct" that event. I cannot go into my reasons for this scepticism here (see Taylor 1997: 19–21), and, in any case, I sympathize with the more general idea which I take to motivate such claims. For, it does *matter* how people characterize what happened – or rather, it *can* matter. It can matter to the event's participants or to those who observed its occurrence. It can matter to those who hear, read, or think about what happened at a later time. It can matter to the people—historians or others—who are characterizing the historical event in those terms. And it can matter more than one might naively assume that the *verbal designation* of an event could matter. At the same time, we must not overlook the fact that it can matter in what would seem to be an endless variety of ways. This is one of the reasons why I am unhappy with speaking of language as "constituting" or "constructing" the event. Those are catch-all terms that do no justice to the variety and complexity of ways that how an event is spoken or written about can matter to various people in various circumstances. "Constructing" and "constituting" make the way in which the verbal characterization matters sound too consensual, too homogeneous, even too context-independent.

Now consider a third kind of important question about language and history. What account should historians take of the various kinds of rhetorical relationship that hold between the intellectual discourse of "History with a capital H" and the lay discourse of ordinary members of the relevant culture who state (as we say) "in their own words" what happened? This general question about lay and intellectual discourses about history raises a number of more specific issues. But let us focus on one in particular: What difference does it make if the history-writing is produced by historians who live in and are members of a different culture from those who were part of what happened? If we grant the general point that how an event is spoken about matters to various constituencies, then what account should be taken of the differences between how event E was characterized at the time that it occurred and how today's historian characterizes it? To connect this back to the preceding question: Is the way that today's historian reflexively "constructs" the historical event different from the way it was reflexively "constructed" at the time, by the members of the culture in which that event took place? Does that difference matter, and how in particular should the historian take account of that difference in her own discourse?

* * *

I have raised three different-but-related questions about the conjunction of language and history. The question on which the rest of this paper will focus incorporates aspects of all three of these initial questions. Before stating this question, it would help first to bring to mind the kind of historical circumstances whose occurrence is typically reported in utterances using *verba dicendi*, that is, "verbs of saying" or speech act verbs. In other words, I am speaking of historical events which might be reported by saying that:

- S promised to H to do X
- S threatened to do X
- S reported to H that P
- S mentioned that P
- S warned H that P
- S okayed H's proposal
- S thanked H
- S invited H to P
- S congratulated H
- S boasted that P
- S admitted that P
- S insisted that P
- S lied that P

In some languages there are also nouns which correspond to their verbs of saying: thus, for example, in English one can speak of a promise, a threat, a report, a lie, a boast, a warning, etc. In sum, I am speaking of historical events

1 in which language plays an integral part,
2 the cultural significance of which, under one theorized manner-of-speaking, is at least in part "constructed" by the verb of saying, and
3 which present interesting rhetorical problems for those who would represent such events in intellectual discourse.

How should the historian (or the linguist or the discourse analyst, for that matter) characterize such events? For events of this type, how should he say "what happened"? This question should be of triple interest to historians and any others who reflect on the theoretical implications of historical discourse.

In addressing the question I have just raised, certain factors must be taken into account. In the first place, we must keep in mind that verbs of saying are not linguistic or cultural universals. Notwithstanding some arguments (Wierzbicka 1996) claiming that there are in fact a few universal verbs of saying, it is abundantly clear from ethnographic studies (e.g. Stross 1974, Silverstein 1985, Verschueren 1985, Agar 1994) that different languages—different cultures—have vastly different inventories of such terms. Language 1 may have many more verbs of saying than Language 2. Language 2 may have no way of expressing the meaning of one or more of Language 1's verbs of saying. The set of verbs of saying in Language 2 may not be isomorphic with the equivalent set in Language 1, with a variety of gaps, *mésalliances*, asymmetries, and *faux amis* that are detectable only on comparative analysis. Furthermore, it is no less clear that one and the same languaculture (to borrow Michael Agar's (1994) terminological blend) will change its verbs of saying over time: change, that is, both the inventory of verbs and their meanings.

This relativism of verbs of saying suggests a complication for the historian: the historian's languaculture today may not have in its inventory the verb of saying that a member of the contemporary languaculture would have used to report what happened. In this case we must ask: how should the historian characterize the event? Should he use one of his own culture's verbs of saying even though it was not part of the languaculture's inventory at the time of the reported event? Or should he use the verb of saying that the culture's own members would have used at that time, even though this verb of saying does not exist in the historian's present-day languaculture? And what are the implications of each of these options?

There is a second important factor that we must take into account in considering the question of the use of verbs of saying to characterize historical speech events. Verbs of saying have important and culture-specific significance. Much of the time when, in English, we report what happened between a speaker and a hearer, we do so using a verb of saying: that is, we say something like S promised to H to do X; then H insulted S; whereupon S confessed to H that P, and H replied that Q, and so on. The metalinguistic framing of such reports can both draw on and influence cultural understanding. Without going too far down the "language-constitutes-experience" road, we can still make sense of the claim that much of our understanding of what happens in interpersonal communication is filtered through our language's *verba dicendi*. At the very least we have to accept that we talk about speech events using verbs of saying (and their related nouns) and *that it is by means of such talk* that we inform others of, negotiate responses to, raise questions about, express objections to, discuss the implications of, and provide a justification for speech events – as well as make comparisons and other kinds of connections between two or more speech events. In other words, our verbs of saying are tools whose employment is crucial to the methods by which we in our culture attempt to negotiate the interpersonal significance of what happened in a given speech event or set of speech events.

In considering the cultural significance of verbs of saying—and the differences between one languaculture's verbs of saying and another's—some thought should be given to what is involved in being a competent user of a given verb of saying. For example:

- If you know what it means in English languaculture to say that S promised to H to do P, then you know that, all things being equal, H will now take S to be committed to do P.
- If you know what it means in Chinese languaculture to apologize (Chinese word: *daoqian*), then you know that the person to whom the apology has been addressed has the right to determine if there has been any harm done.
- If you know what it means in American adolescent culture to ask someone for a date or to snitch on someone, then you know that...

One way of putting this general point is that being a competent user of a verb of saying is not just a matter of knowing some atom of meaning or definitional equivalence, but rather of being familiar with a whole web of implications, from the potential to the inevitable, which competent members of the culture are inclined to draw from its use. This means that even if between two languages there is a conventional translational pair of two verbs of saying—say, English *apologize* and French *demander pardon*—one should not assume that the use of each expression in its home languaculture has the same significance. While what is termed the two expressions' "lexical meanings" may conventionally be said to be "the same", still, the web of implications that the use of each draws on could be very different. This also applies, of course, to the pairing of the "apologize" of renaissance English with the "apologize" of American English today.

A further implication of this line of discussion is that simply using another culture's or another time period's *own* verb of saying in reporting a speech event is not enough to avoid the problems raised here. For the reader of the report will need much more background, cultural information, etc. if she is to understand the cultural significance of that report; what that report would mean (in the much fuller, cultural-implicational, sense of that term) to the members of the relevant languaculture. Consider, for example, telling an American audience that 'Harold gave his word to William that P.' One has to know a lot more about medieval culture to understand the implications—cultural significance—of such a claim. We might at least begin by asking what it meant to give one's word in Harold's time and in what ways this is similar to or different from what the implications might be of giving one's word in contemporary American culture.

Rather than continue this somewhat unstructured list of the various kinds of anxieties which one might have in using verbs of saying to report historical speech events, I would like to shift the focus to the consideration of the arguments of a leading school of linguistic anthropologists, grouped around Michael Silverstein, which has claimed that there is crucial theoretical importance to the question of what social scientists should make of folk linguistic expressions.

> In the course of field work, linguists, like other anthropologists, spend a great deal of time listening to people talk about what they are doing. The resulting data form a corpus of speech about speech, a "meta-corpus" as it were, that consists of speech at the same time that it seems to talk about, or characterize, speech as a meaningful social action. In reply to our queries or spontaneously, people will utter descriptive statements about who has said or can say what to whom, when, why, and

where, just like statements about who can give presents of certain kinds to whom, when, why, and where. But talking about "saying" is, for better or worse, also an example of "saying"; and such metalanguage, for the analyst of culture, is as much a part of the problem as part of the solution. As is readily apparent, all our efforts to differentiate "conscious native models" from "anthropologist's models," or "ethnotheories" and "ideologies" from "objective social reality," are attempts to come to grips with the metalanguage vs. language relationship, or its more general form, (meta-)language vs. action. (Silverstein 1981: 1)

* * *

Perhaps the central concept in Silverstein's extensive theory of language is that of 'metapragmatics':

> If we take *pragmatics* to be the phenomenon of sign usage in communicative situations, then *metapragmatics* is the metalinguistics that describes such pragmatics. Not surprisingly, metapragmatic usage in a language frequently centers on seeming ... functional descriptors of what people use the language for, constituting a lexical set of verbs of saying (*verba dicendi*). (Silverstein 1985: 133)

Silverstein and his colleagues have published widely on the kinds of metapragmatic features that they have identified in the discourses of different cultures and on the kinds of communicative functions that these metapragmatic features can be seen to serve. Arguing from a theoretical model that Silverstein has developed over the past three decades, combining Peircean semiotics with Prague School functionalism and Whorfian ethnolinguistics, he and his colleagues argue that the metapragmatic features of discourse, in their view, extend far beyond the verbs of saying that first come to mind. On the premise that metapragmatic forms all signify something about what is or was an ongoing communicational situation, Silverstein and his colleagues include in the class of metapragmatic features a wide variety of indexical forms that includes, for example, first- and second-person pronouns, demonstratives like *this*, *that*, and *those*, tense and aspect indicators, prosodic structure, and more. Given my focus in this essay, I will confine my attention in most of what remains to what Silverstein and his colleagues have to say about verbs of saying.

It is noteworthy that, unlike the vast majority of orthodox linguists, Silverstein does not treat the metapragmatic function of language as a supplementary add-on to language's more common-and-garden communicational functions. On the contrary, Silverstein takes the metapragmatic function to be essential to language: in particular, he sees it as necessary for the coherence and interpretability of interactional discourse. Loosely put, his claim is that it is only because we talk about contextualized linguistic activities—and conceptualize them accordingly—that those activities can serve as effective means of communication. In a 1993 paper, he states:

> Without a metapragmatic function simultaneously in play with whatever pragmatic function(s) there may be in discursive interaction, there is no possibility of interactional coherence ... (. . .) Understanding discursive interaction as events of such-and-such type is precisely having a [metapragmatic] model of interactional text. (Silverstein 1993: 36)

In other words, Silverstein claims that discursive interaction is only possible because, among other things, speakers and hearers conceive of what-is-going-on as consisting in events of particular types; they impose a metapragmatic model on their and their interlocutors' contributions to the developing interaction. The "smoothness of coherent discursive interaction" would be impossible without this kind of metapragmatic regimentation (Silverstein 1993: 48). One of Silverstein's colleagues at the University of Chicago, John Lucy, puts this point even more starkly, declaring that "reflexive (or metapragmatic) activity is essential to language use." (Lucy 1993a: 18)

While verbs of saying – which exist in every language – are just one of the many kinds of metapragmatic feature that populate discourse, nevertheless, according to Silverstein they have a special importance. For it is by means of its verbs of saying that a community's conceptualization of the event structure and purposivity of linguistic activity is constructed – in other words, their metapragmatic model of what happens in verbal interaction. This conceptualization amounts to what Silverstein calls a "cultural ideology of language" or a "folk metapragmatics". In turn, Silverstein holds that how a culture conceptualizes linguistic activity influences the ways in which that culture's speakers conceive of contributing to verbal interactions, the ways in which they do in fact contribute to those interactions, and the interpretive means by which hearers make sense of their contributions. In other words, a culture's metapragmatic ideology not only influences how its members *conceptualize* language-in-use but also how they *participate in* its ongoing practices: in particular, how they integrate acts of speech into their interactional activity.

Furthermore, it is because a culture's verbs of saying serve to construct its members' folk metapragmatic ideology that Silverstein says that these verbs give linguists, anthropologists, and others

> an empirical entree into the conceptual understanding of language that each society of speakers brings to bear on the activity of actually using it .... In other words, there is a necessary relationship between the way in which metapragmatic constructions of languages code the pragmatics of speaking, and the ideological and cognitive strategies that speakers employ in culturally-conceptualized situations of speaking, i.e., in their [purposive use] of language. (Silverstein 1985: 138)

This view of folk metapragmatic ideology is related to a more general theoretical premise underlying the work of Silverstein's school. Linguistic interaction is taken to be a dialectic between signs and interactional context, but, crucially, a dialectic which is mediated by language ideology. For it is a culture's metapragmatic ideology which informs its members' purposive use of signs to respond to and contribute to ongoing interactional circumstances. "Ideology and praxis reinforce each other . . ." (Silverstein 1979: 210).

It is clear, then, that Silverstein and his colleagues attribute great importance to folk metapragmatic discourse and to its constituent terms and expressions, such as its verbs of saying. In this case, one may be surprised to learn that Silverstein and his colleagues are at best ambivalent about the role that metapragmatic expressions should have in the *study* of language and discourse – that is to say, in the subfield of linguistics called *pragmatics*.

> [H]ow fraught with danger is our taking at face value any statements by participants about various pragmatically-meaningful actions... (Silverstein 1981: 20)

Why, one wants to ask, would it be "fraught with danger" to take at face value a participant's claim, say, that he had promised to do something? Or that he had apologized? Or that he had been teasing? Or that he had been complaining? Silverstein's answer is that native participant testimony is a kind of "metabehavioral interpretation", that is, an "ethnosociology" with a folk-metapragmatic component (Silverstein 1976: 52), and that the view from this perspective does not necessarily correspond with "what the natives are really doing" (Silverstein 1976: 23). His support for this sceptical judgment is that "natives' understanding of their own systems of linguistic usage frequently conflicts" with the understanding of their behavior that can be developed from (a more objective) linguistic perspective (Silverstein 1979: 208). In a 1976 paper he laments:

> I think that every fieldworker has had such experiences, where a careful sorting out of kinds of pragmatic effects ultimately just cannot rely on the metapragmatic testimony of native participants. (Silverstein 1976: 49)

What are Silverstein's objections to folk metapragmatics, in particular to verbs of saying? He spells out these objections in a series of articles published in the late 1970s and early 1980s in which he criticizes John Austin's theorizing of speech acts and of the various kinds of "acts" and "forces" which Austin conjures up to explain how we do things with words.

Silverstein claims that, from the native folk-ideological point of view, performative formulae such as "I promise you that P"

> seem to accomplish, to 'do', some specific predicated transformations of the social relations and other contextual understandings in the situation of speech . . ." (Silverstein 1979: 209)

For example, folk ideology takes the utterance of the performative formula 'I promise you that . . .' to place the speaker "in some new understood relationship of obligation to the addressee." The utterance of the performative formula—given the satisfaction of certain prerequisites—is, in and of itself, the 'doing' of a kind of conventionally recognized act. This is the act of promising. The uttering of various other performative formulae—again, given the satisfaction of the relevant contextual conditions—constitutes the performance of other kinds of illocutionary acts, such as apologizing, baptizing, ordering, betting, warning, etc. Austin calls these kinds of communicational acts "illocutionary acts". These *acts* are the product of the illocutionary *forces* which, Austin claims, the performative formulae have when used in context.

However, Silverstein argues that the concept of the illocutionary act, like that of illocutionary force, is an illusion. There are no such things as illocutionary acts or forces. Instead, these so-called acts and forces are mythical objectifications of folk metapragmatic discourse. In other words, to take a step back for a moment to this chapter's overarching theme, Silverstein claims that the kinds of speech acts which are commonly reported in historical discourse—promises, apologies, insults, giving one's word, warnings, etc.—are merely the illusory figments of folk imagination; moreover, the folk imagination of a particular languaculture at a particular historical moment in time. In other words, not only are verbs of saying culturally dependent and variable, they also stand for phenomena which are only the illusory figments of a culture's folk-linguistic imagination. If this is true, then it is clear that there is even more justification for the historian or linguist to be wary of using verbs of saying in reporting historical speech events:

> [L]inguistics has characteristically taken at face value a native ideology that objectifies "force" in language itself, concretizing this force in terms of propositional-structure-as-usual. Social anthropological studies have characteristically analyzed native ideology as though it were an accurate "scientific" picture of the relation of language form to social context. Both of these...are expectable in terms of a broadened understanding of the bases of ideology that Whorf proposed, especially as such broadened understanding explains the tendency to assimilate our own "scientific" views to the source from which they have emerged, our own European folk ideology of language. (Silverstein 1979: 204)

However, before we can weigh up the implications of Silverstein's argument, we need to look more closely at its grounding in Silverstein's analysis of how Austin was fooled into believing in the existence of illocutionary acts and forces. "Where," Silverstein asks, "do Austin's ideas come from about the nature of these 'acts' and the 'forces' and 'effects' they embody?" (Silverstein 1979: 210). Their origin lies in the objectification of "particular ways of reporting 'what happened' in an event of using language" (Silverstein 1979: 211) – in particular, in the "projection of cryptotypic selective categories of lexical forms in typical metapragmatic discourse" (Silverstein 1979: 210). The following is an abbreviated explanation of Silverstein's reasoning.

Silverstein says that native metapragmatic ideology has a tendency to "rationalize the pragmatic system of language...with an ideology of language that centers on the surface-segmentable items" of propositionally interpreted sentences (Silverstein 1979: 208). Thus, native metapragmatic ideology tends to locate the pragmatic effectiveness of language-in-context in particular words, phrases, and similar surface-segmentable items of sentences. For instance, native ideology focuses on the surface-structure similarity (i.e. cryptotypic relationship) between indirect quotations like

a "He said that he will buy the house," and

b "He promised that he will buy the house"

Both of these sentences describe a speech event, and, because the framed construction

"—— that he will buy the house"

is the same in both cases, native ideology rationalizes that "promising is really saying... plus something else" (Silverstein 1979: 213). In other words, it identifies a relationship of *hyponymy* between the two lexical forms *say* and *promise* and concludes that

> ... this relationship reflects a real inclusion relationship at the level of what happened. (Silverstein 1979: 213)

It is therefore merely a matter of following native ideology when Austin reasons that an utterance like "I promise that I will buy the house" consists in the rhetic act of my asserting a particular propositional content—that I-will-buy-the-house—plus the illocutionary act of *promising*. Note that the reasoning proceeds from a perceived cryptotypic relationship at the surface level of utterances to an assumed pragmatic relationship at the level of the communicational act itself.

Second, native ideology focuses on the surface structure analogy between the metapragmatic reports

c "He promised that P,"

on the one hand, and, on the other,

> d "He joked that P"
> "He complained that P"
> "He answered that P"
> "He explained that P"
> "He threatened that P"
> "He boasted that P"
> "He exclaimed that P",
> and so on.

Note that while (c) "He promised that P" could be a report of the utterance of a grammatically related performative formula "I promise that P," the reports under (d) could not. There are no performative formulae in English such as "I explain that P" or "I joke that P" or "I answer that P" or "I threaten that P" or "I boast that P" to relate in the same way to the third-person reports under (d). Nevertheless, on the basis of the perceived cryptotypic pattern between "He promised that P" and the other third-person metapragmatic reports under (d), native ideology suggests that—like promising—joking, complaining, explaining, threatening, boasting, etc., are also kinds of illocutionary acts: pragmatic add-ons to the rhetic act of expressing a propositional content. And, by extending this reasoning to similar analogies between other kinds of metapragmatic reports, native ideology also concludes that teasing, insulting, whining, appealing, asking for, bragging, justifying, thanking, emphasizing, etc., etc., are further kinds of illocutionary forces that an utterance might have. The fact that, in contrast with "He promised that P," these others do not have related explicit performative formulae is explained away by assuming that the performance of these illocutionary acts is always "indirect". That is, their illocutionary force has to be deduced from the contextual utterance of a non-explicit sentence.

According to Silverstein, it is this kind of folk-ideology-guided reasoning that leads Austin to declare that every utterance is a laminated form involving a phonetic act, a phatic act, a rhetic act (these last three making up the locutionary act), an illocutionary act and perhaps also a perlocutionary act. But Silverstein's view is that these types of acts are nothing but mythological beasts. Complaining, explaining, joking, teasing, etc.: these are not real acts that an English speaker, or any other kind of speaker, ever produces in verbal interaction. Silverstein grants that it is important to English speakers to *speak* of these acts, and even to design their contributions to linguistic interaction on the premise that such acts regularly occur. But this should not lead the theorist to construct pragmatic theories which attribute a reality to these ideological objectifications of the metapragmatic discourse of English languaculture. Silverstein concludes that "speech-event names" do not "delimit a principled area for 'scientific study'" (Silverstein 1979: 210).

> There is no reason why an ideology that grows piecemeal from various metapragmatic formulations of a language should . . . give adequate analytic insight...
> (Silverstein 1979: 214)

Silverstein has a different explanation of the pragmatic properties of communicational interaction and of the pragmatic function of performative formulae such as 'I promise that P'. This is not the place to go into the details of his pragmatic model. In any case, it is not relevant to the general point that I am trying to raise here concerning what use historians, linguists and anthropologists should make of native metalinguistic characterizations.

However, it is worth looking briefly at what Silverstein says elsewhere about the folk metapragmatics, not of English, but of Chinook, a Native American language formerly spoken near the mouth of the Columbia River, in the northwestern United States. Again, I will not have space to give even a brief sketch of Silverstein's insightful analysis of the various verbs of saying used in Chinook narratives. Needless to say, the metapragmatic forms characterize their framed speech reports in ways that have little if any correspondence to the ways that the familiar English verbs of saying do. But, what is most relevant in the present context is Silverstein's claim that Chinook has no metapragmatic forms that characterize an utterance as an assertion.

> [I]n Chinookan metapragmatic coding...there is no explicit metapragmatic concept of referring-and-predicat-ing as [a purposive function of language] akin to that embodied in our metapragmatic formulae such as "He *asserted* that . . . ," "He *stated* that . . . ," – or even "He *explained* that . . ." Nor is there any text-pragmatic evidence that. . . truth-functional semantic propositionality . . . is of significance to the Chinookan conceptualization of language use as a significant activity. (Silverstein 1985: 169)

Nevertheless, this does not lead Silverstein to conclude that Chinook utterances never assert propositional contents or represent states-of-affair in truth-functional terms. On the contrary, Silverstein maintains that propositionality is implicit in the Chinook narratives and in the Chinookan speech events reported in those narratives (Silverstein 1985: 169). However, propositionality is never a focus of Chinookan metapragmatic discourse; nor is it therefore of significance to the Chinookan conceptualization of language use, since, as we have seen, that conceptualization is derived from the culture's folk metapragmatic discourse.

So, these two examples—English and Chinook verbs of saying—appear to illustrate opposite possibilities. In the case of English, there is a wealth of verbs of saying, but these do not correspond to the real pragmatic properties of English language-in-use (although those verbs have misled speech act theorists into thinking that they do). On the other hand, although Chinook does have verbs of saying, they are not translation equivalents of the English ones. But, even more important is the fact that Chinook does not have a verb of saying that represents a pragmatic feature that *really is*, in Silversetin's view, characteristic of Chinook language-in-use – namely, the production of utterances that assert propositional content. In both cases, a realistic interpretation of their inventory of verbs of saying gives a false picture of the pragmatic properties of language-in-use. Furthermore, given Silverstein's general claims

- that metapragmatic discourse influences speakers' conceptualization of the properties of discursive interaction and, just as important,
- that this in turn influences how they design their own participation in discourse,

we can only conclude that English and Chinook speakers *conceive* of the properties and possibilities of language use in very different ways and that, on the basis of those conceptions, English and Chinook speakers purposively *contribute* to the ongoing production of discourse quite differently as well.

In other words, to put this in more general terms, both the conceptualization of discursive interaction as well as the pragmatic techniques that communicators use to integrate their verbal behavior into particular interactions are culturally variable. Moreover that variation is, at least in part, the product of—that is, are discursively constructed by—the particular properties and patterns of 'folk' metapragmatic discourse in their community. However, notwithstanding this wide range of cultural variability, Silverstein suggests that there are pragmatic properties of discursive interaction which remain unaffected by the cultural vagaries of 'folk' metapragmatic discourse and which are only discoverable by the analytical methods of comparative linguistic research. Chinook speakers *do* assert, even though they never talk about it, and English speakers *do not* in fact produce many of the kinds of speech acts that they frequently talk about in reflexive discourse.

* * *

In an earlier paper (Taylor 2001) I discussed the different positions taken by philosophers and cognitive psychologists regarding the use of what are called "folk psychological" expressions: expressions such as S believes H, S intends to do X, S wishes that P, etc. I opposed one group of theorists, the so-called Eliminativists to two other groups, the Realists and the Anti-Realists. The Eliminativists argue that the expressions of folk psychological discourse should be eliminated from *scientific* discourse about the mind. On the other hand, the Realists and Anti-Realists insist on the *retention* of these expressions in scientific discourse. The Realists and Anti-Realists part company, however, on the issue of the phenomena referred to by folk psychological expressions. The Realists claim that there are real, cognitive phenomena referred to by expressions like "belief", "wish", and "intention", while the Anti-Realists maintain that those expressions have no referents: they seem to stand for something but do not really. Nevertheless, the Anti-Realists argue that because folk psychological expressions have a crucially instrumental function in interpersonal discourse, the Eliminativist's project needs to be resisted. Daniel Dennett, a leading anti-realist, argues that what he calls "the intentional stance"—the lay psychological ideology embodied in folk psychological discourse—is essential to human activity and that to do away with it would be to do away with our ability to understand others and ourselves. And yet surely that ability is part of what cognitive science needs to explain. In other words, eliminating folk psychological expressions from cognitive scientific discourse would mean that cognitive science had no access to the role that self-understanding plays in human psychology. Nevertheless, Dennett does not intend this defense of folk psychological discourse to be taken as an argument in favor of basing the terms of cognitive *science* on those of folk psychological discourse – for those expressions of folk psychological discourse do not in fact refer to anything. On the contrary, while the folk psychological ideology is essential to human psychology and therefore to the subject matter of cognitive science, it should not be taken as a fundamentally accurate view of that subject matter. It is a misleading basis for the scientific theorizing of the human mind.

It might appear therefore that Michael Silverstein's position on folk metapragmatic discourse is analogous to that of the anti-realist Dennett on folk psychological discourse. Just as Dennett claims that the intentional stance—the folk psychological ideology—(i) is essential to human psychology but (ii) is not a firm basis for a scientific appraisal of human psychology, so also Michael Silverstein claims that a culture's metapragmatic ideology (i) is essential to language use in that culture but (ii) is not a solid basis for a scientific appraisal of the true pragmatic properties of their discursive interactions. Without dismissing the *practical* importance of folk psychological concepts and theories to human behavior, Dennett feels that cognitive *science* ought to free itself from the cultural prejudices and idiosyncratic reasoning that it embodies. Similarly, Silverstein feels that a scientifically based pragmatics needs to look both at how language ideologies influence discursive behavior and at the pragmatic realities that are obscured by those culturally specific ideologies.

Where does this leave the historian? What should the historian—or the linguist, for that matter—do with the 'folk' reports of what happened, in particular when the reports in question characterize what happened in terms of a particular kind of speech event? Should such reports—and the psychological and interactional conceptions they embody—be eliminated from professional historical discourse? Should professional historical discourse refrain from using verbs of saying and speech-act names? Or should the use of those items of a culture's reflexive linguistic inventory be treated as an accurate way for the historian to communicate to her audience what really happened? Or should the historian take the anti-realist view, acknowledging the instrumental effectiveness of those expressions for the members' own construction of cultural self-understanding and so also cultural praxis, all the while insisting that those expressions are unsuitable for re-employment in the construction of professional histories? In sum, what relationship should there be between cultural self-understanding and the professional understanding that is the goal of historical discourse?

I realize that this question is hardly a new one for the historian, although I think the particular problem that verbs of saying pose to the history of events-of-speech has not received as much attention in historical discussions as it deserves. At the same time, I believe that modern linguistics remains deeply ambivalent about the role that folk metadiscourse should play in the theorizing of language and discourse. If we look into the foundations of modern linguistic theorizing, we will find, I believe, that this ambivalence has been an ever-present source of rhetorical anxiety and that it has motivated a variety of theoretical acrobatic stunts to counteract its influence. The foundational distinction between 'etic' and 'emic' properties of language is an easily recognizable example of this. As both a reaction to and a continuing source of nourishment for this anxiety the tendency for linguistics has been to proceed as if the problem doesn't really exist or is at least only a background topic that can be ignored in front-line theorizing and description. It is time that this topic were brought once again into the discursive foreground of language theory.

References

Agar, Michael (1994). *Language Shock: Understanding the Culture of Conversation*. New York: William Morrow.

Lucy, John (1993). "Reflexive language and the human disciplines", in J. Lucy (ed.), *Reflexive Language*, Cambridge: Cambridge University Press.

Silverstein, Michael (1976). "Shifters, linguistic categories, and cultural description", in K. Basso and H. Selby (eds.), *Meaning in Anthropology*, Albuquerque: University of New Mexico Press.

Silverstein, Michael (1979). "Language structure and linguistic ideology", in P. Clyne, W.F. Hanks and C.L. Hofbauer (eds), *The Elements: A Parasession on Linguistic Units and Levels.* Chicago: University of Chicago Press.

Silverstein, Michael (1981). *The Limits of Awareness*. Austin: Southwest Educational Development Laboratory. (*Sociolinguistic Working Paper* No. 84)

Silverstein, Michael (1985). "The culture of language in Chinookan narrative texts: or, on saying that ... in Chinook", in J. Nichols and A. Woodbury (eds), *Grammar Inside and Outside the Clause*. Cambridge: Cambridge University Press.

Silverstein, Michael (1993). "Metapragmatic discourse and metapragmatic function" in J. Lucy (ed.), *Reflexive Language.* Cambridge: Cambridge University Press.

Stross, Brian (1974). "Speaking of speaking: Tenejapa Tzeltal metalinguistics" In R. Baumann and J. Sherzer (eds.), *Explorations in the Ethnography of Speaking*. pp.213-239, Cambridge: Cambridge University Press.

Taylor, Talbot J. (1997). *Theorizing Language: Analysis, Normativity, Rhetoric, History*. Oxford: Pergamon.

Taylor, Talbot J. (2001). "Folk psychology and the language myth: what would the integrationist say?", in R. Harris (ed.) *The Language Myth in Western Culture*, pp. 100-117. Richmond: Curzon.

Verschueren, Jef (1985). *What People Say They Do With Words*. Norwood: Ablex.

Wierzbicka, Anna (1996). *Semantics: Primes and Universals*. Oxford: Oxford University Press.

VII

Metalinguistic truisms and the emancipation of the language sciences

Abstract
In his influential critiques of the theoretical foundations of the language sciences, Nigel Love claims that modern linguistics is based on "a cultural metafiction" and that it must "emancipate itself from what is no more than a profoundly important but nonetheless culturally parochial way of construing linguistic phenomena." This paper reviews Love's account of the historical sources and modern consequences of this cultural metafiction and asks why it is so frustratingly difficult to emancipate the language sciences from the epistemological presuppositions of this ethnocentric metafiction. In addressing these questions, the paper explores the accountability of the expert metalinguistic discourse of the language sciences to the normative rhetoric of lay metalinguistic practices – or, in Wittgenstein's distinctive use of the term, to the 'grammar' of those practices.

> "The general form of propositions is: This is how things are." That is the kind of proposition that one repeats to oneself countless times. One thinks that one is tracing the outline of the thing's nature over and over again, and one is merely tracing round the frame through which we look at it. (Wittgenstein, *Philosophical Investigations*, §114)

> One might simply say "O, rubbish!" to someone who wanted to make objections to the propositions that are beyond doubt. That is, not to reply to him but admonish him. (Wittgenstein, *On Certainty*, §495).

1

One of the most important and influential themes in Nigel Love's intellectual and literary career has concerned the need for the modern sciences of language to free themselves from the influence of what he has variously called a "second-order cultural superstructure", namely, Western culture's "metafiction" about language (Love, 2009, p. 34). As he puts it in his paper "On construing the world of language": "Any would-be language science must start by emancipating itself" from this meta-fiction, which "is no more than a profoundly important but nonetheless culturally parochial way of construing linguistic phenomena" (Love, 1995, p. 388).

> [W]hat purports to be a culture-neutral science of language embodies a conceptualization of languages that was already in daily use for purposes of formal linguistic education in the culture whose product that science is. To say the least, that is a remarkable coincidence. (Love, 1995, p. 381)

As described in several of Love's published chapters and articles, the Western cultural metafiction represents speech utterances as superficially diverse manifestations of some portion of an abstract system called "a language". Moreover, it treats that system as something which exists in advance of any actual utterance and which remains invariant across the changing circumstances of actual speech events. "Why should this be so?", Love asks. "It's not as if languages are there for the finding" (Love, 1995, p. 378).

In his writings over the past three decades, Love has provided extensive support for his diagnosis of this cultural metafiction afflicting the language sciences. It is not my intention in this paper to offer additional argument for that diagnosis or for the treatment that he recommends: namely, to emancipate the language sciences from the metafiction. Instead, for the narrower purposes of this paper, I will simply take that diagnosis and recommendation for granted so that I can focus on a follow-up question: Given that other modern sciences (chemistry, anatomy, geology, etc.) have long since emancipated themselves from the culturally parochial fictions which dominated their subjects for centuries, why haven't the language sciences emancipated themselves from their cultural metafiction? After all, the arguments motivating the need for emancipation from this cultural metafiction have been around for at least half a century – not only in Love's influential publications, of course, or indeed in the publications of Love's late mentor, Roy Harris (1981, 1982, 1987) and of the many scholars influenced by Harris, but also in the writings of many other scholars (cf. Baumann and Briggs, 2003; Agha, 2007b; Linell, 2005). These arguments have been expressed often and motivated in a variety of ways. Evidence of many different kinds have been provided in their support. They have been frequently praised and never successfully rebutted – indeed rarely explicitly critiqued. So why haven't the language sciences emancipated themselves from the cultural metafiction to which they are apparently enslaved?

What I will argue is that such an emancipation is much more difficult to do than is usually acknowledged. It is, of course, more difficult than simply professing acceptance of Love and others' demonstration of the metafiction's pernicious influence on the language sciences. There is, after all, a difference between being emancipated and asserting that one is. If emancipating the language sciences from their cultural metafiction were that simple, it would have been achieved long ago. The source of the difficulty, I will argue, is not well-recognized, let alone sufficiently studied and understood. To succeed in emancipating the language sciences from the cultural metafiction to which they are enthralled, we need to look more closely at how that metafiction maintains such a forceful grip on discourse in the language sciences.

2

Before addressing this topic, it will help to provide an overview of the distinctive features of the metafiction. This can most easily be done by paraphrasing Love's account of the metafiction's historical emergence and subsequent development in Western culture. Love (1995) locates the metafiction's source in the tools and practices developed for the instrumental purposes of pedagogical grammar, as used in the Western educational tradition since classical antiquity. "[I]t is traditional grammar that has bequeathed to modern linguistic science its commitment to the idea that behind speech there are objects called 'languages'." (Love, 1995, p. 380)

> For the traditional grammarian a language consists of a fixed inventory of microunits (words) displayed in a dictionary as a set of correspondences between forms and meanings, which are combinable into macrounits

(sentences) according to the rules laid out in a grammar book. The network of ideas underlying traditional grammar involves imposing on the continuum of linguistic differences between people at different times and places an analysis in terms of discrete linguistic systems (languages). Traditional grammar abstracts from interactive behavior deemed to involve a given such system what it sets up as the strictly linguistic aspects of that behavior. It then projects this abstraction as a body of knowledge which, if acquired by a learner, might be put to use in interactive episodes with existing speakers of the language in question. (Love, 1995, p. 380)

Love identifies some of the most important implications of the traditional pedagogue's conception of a language (1995, pp. 380–385):

- A language is an object and language-use is a form of behavior secondary to that object.
- Language use is founded on, and only possible because of, knowledge of the object.
- Utterances consist in the instantiation of abstract and invariant elements of the language.
- The acceptability of linguistic expressions solely concerns "a dimension of 'pure linguisticity' ... (sometimes called 'grammaticality') that potential utterances either have or do not have in the abstract". (Love, 1995, pp. 381–382).
- A language is a closed and homogenous system. The grammar book and the dictionary comprise the whole language: a totality which may in principle be known perfectly.

An important stage in this history occurs in the Renaissance, when this pedagogically-inspired conception of a language came to be exploited for the nationalist project of creating, codifying, and institutionalizing standardized written languages for the populations of the emerging European nation-states (cf. also Harris, 1981).

> The Western concept of a language has for historical reasons been intimately bound up with ideas about nationhood and nationalism. Western nation states have in different degrees found it desirable to propagate authoritatively codified 'standard' languages disseminated to linguistically more or less heterogeneous populations through formal education. Hence a prescriptivist discourse about language conducted by a subset of the state's citizens who have come to be appointed guardians of the purity of its official language, with consequent marginalization of the language of everyone else. This is clearly a non-essential feature, or complex of features, of one particular linguistic culture. It is perhaps surprising, or at any rate worth noting, that such a feature should be so faithfully mirrored in the linguistic science sponsored by this culture. (Love, 2009, p. 44)

The culminating stage in the metafiction's historical genealogy came in the nineteenth and twentieth centuries with the emergence, and eventual disciplinary formalization, of the descriptive and explanatory discourses of the language sciences. The traditional grammarian's conceptualization of a language—now authoritatively institutionalized and educationally disseminated—provided for these fledgling sciences a ready-made fund of puzzling, foundational questions to serve as subjects for scientific research and theoretical inquiry.

- What is *a language* – such as the English language or the Mohawk language?
- What it is for someone to *know* a language?
- What is it for two people—or, indeed, for several million people—to know *the same language*?
- What is it for a speaker *to use* a language in an actual speech event, or for a hearer to use it to understand what is said?
- What it is for parts of distinct, transient utterances each to be instances of one of the language's *words*?
- What is it for the word *hand* to mean what humans have at the end of their arms – or for the word *fortnight* to mean 'two weeks'?
- What it is for a speaker's utterance of "the pope" to *refer* to a religious leader who lives in Rome?
- What it is for a hearer to *understand* what a speaker says?
- What is it for the utterance "My stomach hurts" *to be true*?
- How do children learn such linguistic things as *languages* and words?
- How did early humans develop such linguistic things?

3

The past decades have shown that emancipation from the Western cultural metafiction is stubbornly difficult to achieve. Why? To address this question, I will suggest the adoption of a different, yet complementary, account of the metafiction's hold on the language sciences from the account given in historical genealogy just sketched. I begin by giving a paraphrased sampling of the type of responses addressed to me when—speaking to students, colleagues, or interested non-academics—I have expressed scepticism about one or other of the components of the cultural metafiction.

- "You deny, Dr. Taylor, that there are such things as languages and that speakers and hearers use a language when they speak. Yet, the conversation we are currently having is in the English language, isn't it? And if we were speaking Danish, Zulu, or Chinese, wouldn't we be using one of those languages?"
- "You claim that a language is not something that anyone actually knows. Yet, while I don't know the Japanese language, there are millions who do, aren't there?"
- "You assert that people don't communicate by using a language. Yet, it's because we are using the English language right now that you and I are able to understand each other, isn't it? For if we weren't using the same language, we wouldn't be able to understand each other, right?"
- "You say there's no such thing as parts of different utterances being instances of the same word. Yet didn't you these past few minutes utter the same English word *language* several times?"
- "You say that it's a cultural fiction that words have meanings. But the word *fortnight* means 'two weeks', doesn't it? And (*holding hand up*), doesn't *hand* mean THIS?"
- "You deny that people ever understand what others say. But you understood what I just said, didn't you?

Among those scholars who have openly expressed a commitment to the emancipation of linguistic inquiry from its cultural metafiction, I doubt that there are any who haven't had such responses thrown back at them when expressing scepticism about components of the Western cultural metafiction. No less telling, I am sure that there are many of us who have found *ourselves* silently voicing such responses when, say, thinking through an argument for an upcoming conference talk or for an article we are working on, or when writing up a proposal for a publisher or grant agency, or when, after a year teaching introductory linguistics to our students, we puzzle about how best, in year two, to come out of the disciplinary closet to explain our deep scepticism about, indeed outright rejection of, much of what we taught them the first year.

At these moments, we may feel like we are standing in something like a dialogical *cul de sac*. One voice inside is pressing us forward in denial of this or that component of the Western cultural metafiction, but another immediately replies with mutually supporting commonplaces that together seem to close off the road ahead with something like a metalinguistic brick wall. In my case, what this familiar experience has taught me is the need to inquire more closely into the composition of the bricks.

4

In initiating such an inquiry, it may help to consider the following three points. First, it is worth noting that these familiar responses are often formulated as rhetorical questions. A rhetorical question is typically characterized as presupposing the truth of an obvious (or 'understood') answer to the question. So, for instance, Shylock's rhetorical questions "If you prick us, do we not bleed? If you tickle us, do we not laugh?" presuppose the truth of the understood answers "Yes, you bleed" and "Yes, you laugh". The metalinguistic rhetorical question "Doesn't *hand* mean this?", said by a speaker waving her hand in front of your face, presupposes the truth of the 'understood' commonplace "*Hand* means this". And the rhetorical question "There are millions who know and use the Japanese language every day, aren't there?" presupposes the obvious truth of "There are millions who know and use the Japanese language every day".

Second, the obvious ('understood') nature of such commonplace responses to linguistic scepticism is an indication of their normative character. What do I mean by this? One way to foreground the normativity of such metalinguistic commonplaces is to imagine a doppelgänger of the ethnomethodologist Harold Garfinkel who, carrying out one of his famous 'breaching' experiments, goes through the day expressing his denial of familiar metalinguistic commonplaces.

> NN: "Don't you understand what I'm saying?"
> Garfinkel: "No, I don't. There is no such thing as understanding what someone says. In fact, no one actually ever understands anything said to them".

> NN: (*holding hand up*) "Doesn't *hand* mean THIS?"
> Garfinkel: "No, *hand* doesn't mean THAT. It doesn't actually mean anything."

> NN. "Aren't we talking right now in the English language?"
> Garfinkel: "No we are not. There are no such things as languages."

> NN. "When I say that my name is Nancy, what I'm saying is true, isn't it?"
> Garfinkel: "No, there is no such thing as an utterance being true (or false). For that matter, there is no such thing as a name either."

Getting increasingly desperate, the commonsense interlocutor might say:

> NN. "Look, Harold. Can't we at least agree on this basic, undeniable linguistic fact: namely, that I am

talking about the linguist Nigel Love, emeritus professor at the University of Cape Town?"
Garfinkel. "No, my naïve friend. The fact is that you are not talking about anyone or anything – and so, *a fortiori*, not some recently retired Cape Town professor. There simply is no such thing as talk being *about* anything or anyone."

Whenever anyone utters a commonplace metalinguistic remark about meanings, words, languages, understanding, saying (something) again, the truth or falsity of what someone says, etc., Garfinkel pointedly denies it. He never gives the slightest indication that his metalinguistic breaching is being done for experimental purposes. Further, imagine that this metalinguistic Garfinkel performs his breaching experiment not just for a few awkward hours, but for days, for weeks ... for the rest of his life.

The students who, for a few hours, act out Garfinkel's breaching experiment often report how psychologically stressful and disorienting it is to do so – and how it poses a disturbing challenge to their own sense of personal, moral, and social identity (Garfinkel, 1967). Surely a similar disorientation would occur if the focus of the breaching experiment were metalinguistic discourse – and immeasurably more so if our brave experimenter continued his metalinguistic breaching without a break for years on end.

It is worth reflecting on the difficulties that his breaching behavior would create in routine interactions at work, at school, in commercial settings, and in dealings with the police, administrative offices, or with the legal system. But no less challenging would be his daily, commonplace interactions with friends, neighbors, family members, new acquaintances indeed – with everyone in or outside his familiar communicational community. In permanent metalinguistic rebellion, how could he integrate his life into that of the sociocultural world around him? How could we integrate our lives with his? For instance, who could put up with him—and for how long?—given that he always expresses his denial whenever an interlocutor claims that what was just said is the same as what was said before, or that the two utterances mean, or do not mean, the same, or that they are about this person, event, idea, or object, or that they are true (or false)? It is hard to conceive how one could interact with him in simple, culturally-foundational activities, such as

– having a conversation
– making a plan
– having an argument
– relating a joke
– formulating a joint decision
– evaluating whether what someone does is or isn't what they were told to do
– questioning or supporting the sense, implication, or truth of someone's assertion or reasoning
– assessing whether what someone said would happen is indeed what does happen

In sum, his metalinguistic breaching behavior would make it impossible for him to be a participant in the kind of everyday interactions that make up our daily social lives. To make things even worse, if one attempted to discuss his breaching behavior with him and its social and interactional consequences, his persistent metalinguistic eliminativism would ensure that such efforts would fail as soon as they began.

A: Harold, you are driving your friends and colleagues crazy and making yourself impossible to live or work with. For everyone's sake, you have to stop denying it each time anyone says anything about language.

Garfinkel: I don't do that. There is no such thing as denying what someone says.

It would seem inevitable that, perhaps after several well-intentioned interventions—which would increasingly be made by medical and legal authorities—our metalinguistic Garfinkel would ultimately be incarcerated or removed in some other way from social life. We count on each other to participate cooperatively in metalinguistic practices, from the most mundane and commonplace to those that are required to sustain our social and cultural institutions. And we are well aware that our fellow community members count on us for the same.

Another way of foregrounding the normativity of meta-linguistic commonplaces would be to assimilate them to the "bedrock judgments of the obvious" (Williams, 2010) and "hinge certainties" (Moyal-Sharrock, 2016) to whose normative role Wittgenstein returned to frequently in his later writings, most notably in the posthumously published *On Certainty* (1969). In her discussion of the role of such normative certainties in the child's socialization into language, Meredith Williams uses the analogy of calibrating a measuring device such as a yardstick or meter bar. When the stick or bar has been appropriately scored according to our community's norms of measurement, it becomes an integral part of the normative practices within which we derive judgments of the length of objects: for example, judging this wooden plank, this plastic pipe, and that steel beam to be the same length. Analogously, Williams argues, Wittgenstein represents the child's communicational behavior as receiving "calibration" within the scaffolded learning environment. As a consequence, the child comes to produce normative, bedrock judgments within language-games concerning objects, events, actions, experiences, and so on. That is, she calls THIS and THIS "red" but THAT "purple"; she calls THIS a "dog" but THAT a "wolf"; and she says that THIS event and THIS event are "getting dressed", while THAT event is "getting undressed", and so on. Such paradigmatic judgments express normative criteria of acceptability within our everyday language-games.

> Initiate learning is a time of calibration, in which we acquire the skills and techniques to make judgments of normative similarity that constitute the bedrock we share with our fellows. (Williams, 2010, p. 314)

Williams points out that such normative judgments must be treated as beyond justification or falsification – as taken for granted, obvious, a matter of course. "If one cannot believe and act on these judgments, one cannot learn what things are called or learn to calculate or to do science or history. (Williams, 2010, p. 255). Yet as Wittgenstein makes clear in *On Certainty*, this bedrock status is not a matter of epistemic certainty. They are not factual assertions of which we have certain knowledge, but rather are utterances which we hold exempt from doubt because of the normative role they have in our language-games – language-games which, in turn, have a foundational role in our cultural lives within a world of things, persons, events, actions, and experiences. Discussing philosophical debates between epistemological realists and sceptics, Wittgenstein uses the metaphor of door hinges:

> [The] questions that we raise, and our doubts, depend on the fact that some propositions are exempt from doubt, are as it were like hinges on which those turn.

(...) If I want the door to turn, the hinges must stay put." (Wittgenstein, 1969, §341 & §343)

[If] I were to say "It is my unshakeable conviction that etc.", this means ... that I have not consciously arrived at the conviction by following a particular line of thought, but that it is anchored in all my questions and answers, so anchored that I cannot touch it' (Wittgenstein, 1969, §103)

Now I would like to regard this certainty ... as a form of life. But that means I want to conceive it as something that lies beyond being justified or unjustified; as it were, as something animal. (Wittgenstein, 1969, §§358–359)

In Taylor (2013), I argue that, at the same time that the child is being calibrated for objects, colors, social relationships, lengths, events, sensations, and so on – she is also being enculturated into the metalinguistic practices of her community. This involves her calibration for normative judgments of verbal kinds of things, acts, properties, and experiences. Socialization into her community's metalinguistic practices 'scores' the child so that she speaks unreflectingly—not in this case of a "blue" sky or of "five" apples, or of THIS activity as "getting dressed"—but of a certain pattern of behavior as "answering a question" or as "teasing" and another pattern as "asking" or as "doing what S said". She thus comes to measure language as we in her learning environment do: e.g., to call one response to her utterance "understanding" and another response "not understanding", to characterize THIS behavior as "telling" someone something but THAT behavior as "lying" or "meaning [such-and-such]", and to speak of other utterances as "saying [something] again" or as "true" or as "wrong" or as "about what happened" or as "speaking English". Moreover, her acquisition of the community's normative techniques of measuring the component parts, events, activities, experiences, and results of language practices occurs at the same time and in the same learning contexts as does her acquisition of the skills required to participate in the very practices thus metalinguistically measured.

Over time the child will be socialized into increasingly sophisticated metalinguistic practices, ones in which the following sorts of metalinguistic commonplaces will be treated as having a taken-for-granted, normative status.

> Many people know and use the same language as I do, the English language.
> [pɪn] and [pɛn] are different words
> The word *fortnight* means 'two weeks'
> *Margaret* is my name.
> The meaning of *hand* is THIS.
> Instead of "The hamster me bit", you should say "The hamster bit me"
> When people say "the pope" they are talking about a religious leader who lives in Rome
> If you understand what someone says, then you know what they mean.
> It's not true to say that your stomach hurts unless it really does.
> If you say your stomach hurts when it really doesn't, you are lying.

By means of the reflexive enculturation of their communicative practices, children come to take such commonplaces as normative bedrock; and they develop the skills for putting such remarks to productive use in their increasingly proficient integration of their and others' behavior into everyday communicational practices, settings, and cultural ecologies. Moreover, as a child makes ever more sophisticated contributions—productive as well as responsive—to meta-discursive exchanges involving these and other commonplace remarks, the members of her language community take this metalinguistic behavior to satisfy the normative criteria for attributing to her such epistemic accomplishments as knowing "what her name is", "what *fortnight* means", and "what a lie is", knowing "that 'There is no Santa Claus' is true", and knowing "that the language we speak is English but the neighbors' language is Swahili".

Naturally, then, it is no surprise that a metalinguistic Garfinkel—who persists in denying all instances of such metalinguistic 'hinges'—would be objected to, corrected, made fun of, and subjected to personal, moral, and even legal reproaches. And that this would eventually lead to his being socially ostracized and, in all probability, institutionalized.

The third remark I would make about metalinguistic commonplaces is that their normative status also sheds light on their use in what the philosopher Wilfred Sellars (1963) called "language-entry transitions" – discursive transitions from positions outside a language-game to positions within the game. At issue here is the transition from 'folk' (lay) metadiscourse into the expert discourses of the language sciences. Consider, for example, the following imagined—and yet, I assume, recognizably familiar—discursive scenarios.

> **"Given that English and Mohawk (etc.) are languages**, then we need to inquire into the kind of thing that a language is. What is its ontology? Is it natural? Social? Psychological? Abstract? Virtual? What is it for two such things—two languages—to be the same or different? Which of a language's properties are necessary and which contingent? What scientific methods are best suited for describing and explaining those properties?"

"Given that (e.g.) the English language is something that I (and other people) know, then what is it to know a language? Is it a psychological state of mind? A brain state? An ecologically extended or distributed state? How did I—how does anyone—come to know a language? How do whole populations of speakers come to know the same language? How do people put that knowledge to use when speaking or writing, listening or reading?"

"Given that the word *the* is uttered an uncountable number of times every single day, then what is it that makes those acoustically, contextually, geographically, and temporally distinct events all utterances of the same word? What kind of thing is a word (social, psychological, abstract, etc.), such that each of those utterances is a token instance of it? How did the word itself—as distinct from any of those countless utterance events—come into existence? How does it remain in (or disappear from) existence? How is it that speakers and hearers recognize these transient utterance-events as instances of that very same, pre-existing word?"

It isn't hard to imagine the academic fate of an undergraduate Garfinkel who, in his introductory linguistics class, objects to such language-entry transitions. He constantly voices objections to his professor's teaching, denying the premises of all her lectures, assignments, and graded assessments concerning the properties of languages, words and their component sounds, meanings, grammaticality, etc.

"But there are no such things as languages (words, meanings, grammars, etc.)! They are all fictions derived from what is no more than the West's culturally parochial way of construing linguistic phenomena! If we are to be properly trained as apprentices in a truly culture-neutral science of language, this course should be designed to emancipate us from enthrallment to such cultural metafictions! But so far, professor, your class has amounted to nothing more than an exercise in culture maintenance!"

Nor is it hard to imagine an analogous fate being meted out to an equally sceptical assistant professor when presenting her first conference paper at a meeting of the LSA, LAGB, or other scholarly association of language scientists or when submitting her grant application, say, to the National Science Foundation (US) or the European Science Foundation.

My point in inventing these scenarios is to illustrate the normative rhetoric by means of which the bedrock status of commonsense metalinguistic certainties is transferred, largely unnoticed, from the lay metalinguistic practices of (in this case) Anglophone discourse to the epistemologically foundational assumptions, questions, and *explananda* of the expert, professionalized discourse of the language sciences. For, I suggest, it is by those means that normative legitimacy for those assumptions is acquired—and is constantly maintained and enforced—as well as for the scientific enterprises designed to answer those questions and seek those explanations.

5

I have been connecting two distinct but related normative uses of metalinguistic commonplaces in the language sciences. One use is in the policing of the cultural boundaries of the language-games of expert metalinguistic discourse. So, sternly wagging his finger, we might imagine the state trooper warning us: "Say whatever you want, just as long as you don't go beyond the boundaries by denying, say, that English is one language among many thousands in existence, or that different utterances can be instances of the same word or sentence, or that people typically understand each other".

A caveat: it is not of course the case that language science is never permitted any leeway—any looseness of fit—in its normative accommodation to the truisms of lay metalanguage. On the contrary, as theorists of past centuries have repeatedly shown, the metalinguistic police *do* allow the denial of a select few of such commonsense truisms – but only as a necessary sacrifice for the sake of a theory's overall conformity to the body of those truisms. As examples we might cite the denials by Chomsky and Davidson of the existence of languages or Locke's rejection of the assumption that we ordinarily understand each other or Bloomfield's dismissal of the claim that sentences mean by expressing thoughts. However, due to its normative accountability to lay metalanguage, such exceptions are only authorized quite sparingly in language science, like a powerful acid which may be applied in precise drops, here and there; just enough to burn away the weaker parts of theoretical models. But not too much, for that would do more epistemological harm than good.

A second use of commonsense metalinguistic truisms in the language sciences is in providing the taken-for-granted epistemological foundations from which expert metalinguistic inquiry takes its initial discursive steps. In this case we might imagine a research supervisor instructing his students: "Given the existence of languages, words, meanings, grammaticality, etc., your task as scientists-in-training is to explain what such things are, how they are learned by children, how they emerged in human evolution, how they are put to use in communicational exchanges, the nature and limits of their variability within a single speech community, how they change over time, and where they are lodged in the brain, distributed through extended networks, or brought into virtual existence. Now get to work!"

More generally, the point I have been trying to motivate is that—unlike the relation between, say, expert discourse in science of physics and cultural forms of lay discourse about the physical world—expert discourse in the sciences of language is held firmly accountable to the culturally normative status of lay discourse about language. (And, n.b., when I say "lay discourse about language", I am referring, of course, to lay metadiscourse in *Western* culture, Whorf's "Standard Average European", a form of discursive practice which should not be presumed to be anything like a cultural universal. Cf. Agha, 2007a; Lucy, 1993; Silverstein, 1985; Rumsey, 2008, 2015; Webster, 2012). The consequence of expert metalinguistic discourse's accountability to Western-cultural metadiscourse is that a would-be science of language which did not seek to explain, say, what languages or word-meanings are or what it is to mean such-and-such or understand an utterance would be seen to be shirking its fundamental duty as a science.

At the same time, I am not suggesting that this accountability is something which, in doing language science, we should ignore, belittle, or philosophically 'explain away'. On the contrary, we must strive to see it for what it is, an ineliminable component of the cultural-discursive ecology within which the expert metadiscourse of language science must live and make any sense that it is able to make.

6

In approaching my conclusion I return to the question which requires our attention if the language sciences are to try to emancipate themselves from enslavement to Western culture's metafiction. That is, "Why is it that this metafiction has such a powerful hold on discourse in the language sciences?"

One answer to this question—one that I believe to be correct and compelling—is given by the work of Nigel Love and others in which the historical genealogy of the Western cultural metafiction is meticulously traced and analyzed. At the very least, this work offers an illuminating account of the means by which the Western cultural metafiction has developed its institutionalized stranglehold on the language sciences. Such genealogical work is also a powerful illustration of the importance to the language sciences of studying the history of linguistic thought. This is essential not only for understanding the metafictional foundations of the modern sciences of language but also for learning to avoid the garden paths down which the metafiction has led and continues to lead language scientists today. Perhaps most significantly in the present context, it is an invaluable way of motivating the plea to emancipate ourselves from the metafiction's mesmerizing hold.

A second, complementary answer to the question about the cultural metafiction's grip on the language sciences is suggested in sections 4 and 5 above. The focus here is on the accountability of expert metadiscourse to the normative rhetoric of lay metalinguistic practices – or, in Wittgenstein's distinctive use of the term, to the 'grammar' of those practices (Wittgenstein, 1953). This, I propose, is the reason why it is so frustratingly difficult, if not impossible, to emancipate the language sciences from the epistemological presuppositions of the metafiction.

Still, as soon as this second answer is given, another question looms. If the cultural metafiction about language is not only nurtured but robustly defended by the normative rhetoric of lay metafiction, then by what means, if any, can we hope to reduce the metafiction's hitherto unshakeable influence on the language sciences? To address this question I believe that we need to make lay metalinguistic practices a primary topic of research and reflection across the language sciences. Accordingly, I would make the following suggestions, which, in the present context, can at best be only somewhat vague and loosely formulated.

- In order to counter the ethnocentrism at the historical and normative-epistemological core of the language sciences, we should study lay metalinguistic practices in the broadest diversity of cultures and contexts. In doing so, we should draw on all methods, approaches, and techniques available: ethnographic, experimental, observational, conceptual, interactional, 'grammatical', etc. It is by this means that we will have the best chance of bringing to light instances and aspects of metalinguistic activities which, in the better-studied linguistic cultures as well as in those less-well-studied, remain hidden from view within research methodologies which only recognize instances of metadiscourse when a stereotypical metalinguistic expression occurs or when there occurs, in studies of non-Western discourse, an expression which is deemed translatable into one of Western culture's metalinguistic stereotypes (cf. Agha, 2007a).

- We need to study ways that metalanguaging can be seen to play a role in languaging: that is, how metalinguistic practices are dynamically, dialogically, and productively integrated within the broadest range of interactive and contextually-variable communicational circumstances and activities. Examples of such research can be found in Wolf et al. (1996), Rumsey (2008), Hyland (2005), Jaworski et al. (2004), Maschler (2009), and in the papers of Duncker (2017), Hutton (2017), and Jones (2017).

- We need to study how, within the scaffolding environment of initiate learning, children become competent participants in the metalinguistic practices of their linguistic community. Along with their development of ways of doing language, children become increasingly sophisticated participants in their linguistic culture's ways to reflexively engage with that 'doing': to refer to it, to describe it, to ask about it, to explain it, to question it, to provide reasons for it, to correct it, to disagree with it, and so on (to cite only a few of Western culture's metalinguistic practices). Cf. Aukrust (2001, 2004), Stude (2007), Taylor (2010, 2012, 2013) and Perregaard (2017).

- No less important—and yet in certain respects the most challenging of all—we need to try to resist, when studying metalanguage, two compelling yet profoundly misleading tendencies that are at the very core of the metafiction sponsored study of language. For, on the one hand, we would be repeating the error of the metafiction's intellectualism if, abstracting away from their contingent circumstances and normative grammars, we were to construe (to re-entextualize) lay metalinguistic remarks as 'folk', junior-scientific versions of the questions, hypotheses, and assertions at play within the grammar of the language-games of language-scientific discourse (cf. Taylor, 1992; Baumann and Briggs, 2003). On the other hand, we risk repeating the error of the metafiction's representationalism (surrogationalism) if—by introducing elements of the *explanans* into the *explanandum* itself—we construe the expressions we find in either 'lay' or 'expert' metadiscourse as verbally-instantiated representations of underlying or second-order 'somethings': whether abstractions, constructs, concepts, attractors, mental states, virtual objects, etc. (cf. Segerdahl, under review). I suggest, in other words, that we should focus our attention on what people say and do in metalinguistic practices. In our efforts, we should resist the temptation to explain the value of such sayings and doings in terms of the obtaining or non-obtaining of purported states of affairs or entities of which those sayings are true or false representations. Succumbing to that temptation can only, I suggest, lead the study of metalanguage back into the same metafictional thickets in which the modern science of language finds itself entangled.

Lay metalinguistic practices have been largely ignored as a topic in the language sciences – or treated as a peripheral matter outside the central business of linguistic research. *And yet lay metalinguistic practices are a culturally and personally powerful—as well as a necessary and ineliminable—feature of the discursive ecology of the expert metalinguistics of the language sciences.* In the present context, an unfortunate consequence of neglecting the study of lay metalinguistic practices is the undermining of attempts to reduce the authoritative influence of the Western cultural metafiction on the language sciences. And what this means, I have been suggesting, is that linguistic research will continue to be enthralled by the cultural metafiction that both provides the language-entry transitions into the foundational questions of language science and—by wielding the nightstick of their commonsense truisms—polices the boundaries of its permissible answers.

Acknowledgements
I am grateful to Dorthe Duncker, Pär Segerdahl, and Jasper van den Herik who read and provided most helpful comments on early drafts of this paper.

References

Agha, A., 2007a. *Language and Social Relations*. Cambridge University Press, Cambridge.

Agha, A., 2007b. The object called "Language" and the Subject of linguistics. *Journal of English Linguistics*. 35, 217–235.

Aukrust, V.G., 2001. Talk-focused talk in preschools – culturally formed socialization for talk? *First Language* 21, 57–82.

Aukrust, V.G., 2004. Talk about talk with young children: pragmatic socialization in two communities in Norway and the US. *Journal of Child Language*. 31, 177–201.

Baumann, R., Briggs, C., 2003. *Voices of Modernity: Language Ideologies and the Politics of Inequality*. Cambridge University Press, Cambridge, UK.

Duncker, D., 2017. Reflexivity, repetition, and language making online. *Language Sciences*. 61, 28–42.

Garfinkel, H., 1967. *Studies in Ethnomethodology*. Prentice-Hall, New Jersey.

Harris, R., 1981. *The Language-Makers*. Duckworth, London.

Harris, R., 1982. *The Language Myth*. Duckworth, London.

Harris, R., 1987. *The Language Machine*. Duckworth, London.

Hutton, C., 2017. The self and the 'monkey selfie': law, integrationism and the nature of the first order/second order distinction. *Language Sciences*. 61, 93–103.

Hyland, K., 2005. *Metadiscourse: Exploring Interaction in Writing*. Continuum, London.

Jaworski, A., Coupland, N., Galasinski, D., 2004. *Metalanguage: Social and Ideological Perspectives*. Mouton, Berlin.

Jones, P., 2017. Language - the transparent tool: reflections on reflexivity and instrumentality. *Language Sciences*. 61, 5–16.

Linell, P., 2005. *The Written Language Bias in Linguistics*. Routledge, London.

Love, N.L., 1995. On construing the world of language. In: Taylor, J.R., MacLaury, R.E. (Eds.), *Language and the Cognitive Construal of the World*. Mouton de Gruyter, Berlin, pp. 377–389.

Love, N.L., 2009. Science, language, and linguistic culture. *Language and Communication*. 29, 26–46.

Lucy, J., 1993. Metapragmatic presentationals: reporting speech with quotatives in Yucatec Maya. In: Lucy, John A. (Ed.), *Reflexive Language: Reported Speech and Metapragmatics*. Cambridge University Press, Cambridge.

Maschler, Y., 2009. *Metalanguage in Interaction: Hebrew Discourse Markers*. J. Benjamins, Amsterdam.

Moyal-Sharrock, D., 2016. The Animal in epistemology: Wittgenstein's enactivist solution to the problem of regress. In *Hinge Epistemology*, special issue of the *International Journal for the Study of Skepticism*, 6, 97–119.

Perregaard, B., 2017. First-order reality and reflexive practices in children's language development. *Language Sciences*. 61, 64–73.

Rumsey, A., 2008. Confession, anger and cross-cultural articulation in Papua New Guinea. *Anthropological Quarterly* 81 (2), 455–472.

Rumsey, A., 2015. Language, affect and the inculcation of social norms in the New Guinea Highlands and beyond. *Australian Journal of Anthropology*. 26, 349–364.

Segerdahl, P., Critique of pure normativity: taking off the glasses through which metaphysics sees life, (under review).

Sellars, W., 1963. Some reflections on language games. In: *Science, Perception, and Reality*. Humanities Press, New York.

Silverstein, M., 1985. The culture of language in Chinookan narrative texts: or, on saying that . in Chinook. In: Nichols, J., Woodbury, A. (Eds.), *Grammar Inside and Outside the Clause*. Cambridge University Press, Cambridge.

Stude, J., 2007. The acquisition of metapragmatic abilities in preschool children. In: Bublitz, W., Hubler, A. (Eds.), *Metapragmatics in Use*. J. Benjamins, Amsterdam.

Taylor, T.J., 1992. *Mutual Misunderstanding: Scepticism and the Theorizing of Language and Interpretation*. Duke University Press/Routledge, Durham, NC/London.

Taylor, T.J., 2010. Where does language come from? The role of reflexive enculturation in language development. *Language Sciences*. 32/1, 14–27.

Taylor, T.J., 2012. Understanding others and understanding language: how do children do it? *Language Sciences*. 34, 1–12.

Taylor, T.J., 2013. Calibrating the child for language: Meredith Williams on a Wittgensteinian approach to language socialization. *Language Sciences*. 40, 308–320.

Webster, Anthony, 2012. Southern Athapaskan quotative evidentials: a discursive areal typology. In: Seymour, Deni J. (Ed.), *From the Land of Ever Winter to the American Southwest: Athapaskan Migrations, Mobility, and Ethnogenesis*. University of Utah Press, Salt Lake City, pp. 286–302.

Williams, M., 2010. *Blind Obedience: Paradox and Learning in the Later Wittgenstein*. Routledge, London.
Wittgenstein, L., 1953. *Philosophical Investigations*. Blackwell, Oxford.
Wittgenstein, L., 1969. *On Certainty*. Blackwell, Oxford.
Wolf, G., Bocquillon, M., de la Houssaye, D., Krzyzek, P., Meynard, C., Philip, L., 1996. Pronouncing French names in New Orleans. *Language in Society*. 25 (3), 407-426.

Publications of the International Association for the Integrational Study of Language and Communication

2015
David Bade, Rita Harris, Charlotte Conrad. *Roy Harris and Integrational Semiology 1956-2015: A bibliography.*

2020
Sinfree Makoni. *Language in Africa. Selected papers* vol. 1
David Bade. *Efficiencies and Deficiencies: Cataloging and Communication in Libraries.*
Sinfree Makoni. *African Applied Linguistics. Selected Papers*, vol. 2
Sinfree Makoni. *Linguistic Ideologies, Sociolinguistic Myths and Discourse Strategies in Africa. Selected Papers*, vol. 3
Sinfree Makoni. *Languages and Language Planning in Zimbabwe. Selected Papers*, vol. 4.
David Bade. *Integrational Linguistics for Library & Information Science: Linguistics, Philosophy, Rhetoric and Technology.*
David Bade. *Making Mongolians: Linguistics, Historiography, Fiction.*
Lars Taxén. *Exploring the Relation between Biomechanical and Macrosocial Factors: Integrationism meets Neuroscience and Information Systems.*

2021
David Bade. *Epistemologies of Rape and Revelation.*

2022
John Orman. *Indeterminacy and Explanation in Linguistic Inquiry: Contentious Papers 2012 – 2018.*

Adrian Pablé, Cristine Severo, Sinfree Makoni, Peter Jones (orgs.) *Integrationism and Language Ideologies*. (Published in association with Fórum Linguíst!co, Florianópolis, Brasil)

2023

Talbot J. Taylor. *Linguistic Analysis and Normativity. Collected Papers,* vol. 1.

Talbot J. Taylor. *Folk Linguistics, Epistemology, and Language Theories. Collected Papers,* vol. 2.

Talbot J. Taylor. *Children Talking About Talking: The Reflexive Emergence of Language. Collected Papers,* vol. 3.

Talbot J. Taylor. *On the History of Linguistics: Essays of Appreciation and Criticism. Collected Papers,* vol. 4.

Talbot J. Taylor. *Language Origins and Ape Linguistic Research. Collected Papers*, vol. 5.

www.ingramcontent.com/pod-product-compliance
Lightning Source LLC
LaVergne TN
LVHW021238080526
838199LV00088B/4575